# The Generational Wealth System

## A HOLISTIC APPROACH
### to Preserving Your Wealth and Legacy

**Krista McBeath, ChFC®**

McBeath Financial Group
203 Landmark Drive, Unit A
Normal, IL 61761
(309) 808-2224
www.McBeathFinancial.com

# Acknowledgments

This book has been a dream of mine for years. However, I could not have done this without the tremendous support and assistance of my husband, Robert. Robert assists in many areas of our practice, but he does most of his work behind the scenes. With his help, the foundation and principles that I apply within my financial planning practice were translated into book form, creating The Generational Wealth System.

Our inspiration, as you will learn, came from my late father. I undoubtedly inherited my problem-solving skills, love of math, and desire to fix everything from my dad. My mom has greatly shaped my life as well. She has been an excellent role model, leading by example. I learned a lot about business, work ethic, and customer service by watching her and working with her at a young age. Having two self-employed parents helped contribute to my success as an entrepreneur.

I'd be remiss not to thank many fantastic employees. During the most significant expansion years of my business, my dear friend and employee Carol Ambler has been at my side. And over the last year and a half, Lauren Dennewitz has joined us and helped me undertake one of the most extensive changes I've ever made to my firm. I could not do what I do without these two women.

The principles I will discuss in this book are not unique to my firm. I have studied, pursued designations and licenses, and taken more professional exams than I care to count. I also had many mentors over the years who helped guide me, encourage me, and push me to expand my knowledge and areas of practice management.

After leaving my captive insurance agent position in 2007, I opened my own firm and partnered with an insurance marketing organization (IMO) called USA Tax and Insurance, Inc. This firm, led by Stephen Hand, was instrumental in my early years of success. Through their staff, training programs, and a network of peers nationwide, I honed my skills and education in the wealth preservation area. Through this relationship, I was also able to work with

Brokers International, one of the oldest and most influential life insurance, annuity, and wealth planning organizations. In addition, one of my peers, Michael Terrio, became a mentor and friend in a much larger capacity when he later formed Motiv8 Advisors.

My story, and the ideas in this book, are a culmination of years of professional study, financial planning experience, professional relationships, and mentors. I am grateful to each of them.

I hope you enjoy this book and that it opens your eyes to new ideas.

*Krista McBeath*

# Table of Contents

# Introduction

I hate to admit it, but I was a financial advisor for years before I finally realized the driving purpose behind my career choice. I should have seen it all along. I don't think my focus was completely without merit, considering my circumstances, so give me some grace as I explain my path to realizing the full significance and purpose behind my life's endeavor.

I knew I had a calling to the financial services industry to help families. It was a result of seeing the hardship faced by my parents when my dad had health issues. I didn't want other families to face the same thing. So, I made a choice during college to pursue a career in insurance.

When I first began my own company, I focused on financial services such as life insurance, annuities, and tax preparation. I felt it was important to protect people from financial difficulties, and I put my insurance degree to good use.

I also knew that helping people manage and grow their investments could give them greater freedom of choice and help protect their families. So, shortly after, I became an Investment Advisory Representative.

Then it evolved into helping my clients from outliving their retirement funds and giving them a sense of security. I could now help my clients with comprehensive financial planning.

Along the way, I found I had a soft spot for helping widows when they needed financial guidance the most. Then, when it happened to my own mom, I realized first-hand the importance of having someone there when you lose a spouse.

But it wasn't until I became a mother that I understood the full magnitude of financial planning for *families*. My scope of concern had once consisted of merely being adequately insured and allocated appropriately for goals and time horizon. Suddenly, my perspective shifted, and I had a nagging feeling that insurance products and investment portfolios alone inadequately served my clients' needs!

My wake-up moment occurred the first trip my husband and I took without our baby. Jillian was about six months old, and as we prepared to fly out to Las Vegas for an industry conference, I became stricken by panic. *What if we didn't make it back?*

Yes, we were financially comfortable; we each had life insurance and a will. The basics were covered, but if something should happen, how would we *really* know our daughter was taken care of?

And as my mind raced, I reached an epiphany regarding my higher purpose. *It's about our children. It always has been; I just didn't realize it.*

From that moment, I knew I had to do better for her. I not only wanted to provide a secure life while we were here with her, but I also wanted to help prepare for a time – hopefully far in the future – when we wouldn't be here. As I pondered this, I knew that it went even beyond financial and legal preparations. We needed a financial strategy and mentoring for that part of her life. We knew that a well-fleshed-out contingency plan was vital while she was young, but I felt it was also important to protect her from financial hardships later in life. If I could find a way to help her avoid the financial trials I had faced, *why wouldn't I?*

Now, I know some would say facing financial challenges is important so that kids understand the value of money and don't become spoiled brats. We must educate our children about money to help them not make mistakes when they are older, regardless of how many zeroes are in the bank account. What better lessons can we teach than stewardship and strong values for mastering money for ourselves, our family, and for the causes we believe in?

Others might say that by struggling financially, there's a growth process that builds character. I can show plenty of examples of poor people that never experience such maturity. Likewise, there are endless examples of self-made millionaires with little integrity.

Finally, you may have your doubts, because it's common for each new generation to want to provide for themselves and make their own way in the world. But why? Does it really make sense that every generation must start over from square one? Doesn't that say more about the choices the parents and grandparents have made than it being a correct path? Why shouldn't each new generation *build* on the predecessor's successes?

I had gone about the growth in my business completely backward! And then I realized that's how our industry is set up and how most people approach their finances!

Through my own journey, I discovered how backward – and broken – the established financial services industry is.

I knew that I had to provide better for my family first, then my clients and their families. Through writing this book, I hope that I can reach even more people who wish to provide a better foundation for future generations.

# CHAPTER ONE

# Retirement Planning is Broken

A s an industry insider, I've come to the conclusion that many retirees have been systematically failed by the fundamental premise of 'retirement planning.'

Hearing me say that may come as a shock, considering that for years I've been regarded as one of the most prominent financial advisors in my area. Locally I'm known as an instructor at a community college, and I frequently host workshops at the public library. As an author of monthly magazine articles and blog articles, I've been recognized as an authority in financial matters even beyond the local area. My company, McBeath Financial Group, has consistently been voted as the best Financial Planning Firm AND Investment Firm by our local newspaper's readers. Although I still consider myself a young woman, I've got years of formal education and experience in the industry along with some letters behind my name, and I belong to all the right organizations. And yet, the more time I spend helping people prepare for retirement, the more I realize that our industry is often falling short in providing the real help many retirees need.

Before I continue, I want to be very clear. I am not painting individual financial advisors or firms as having bad intentions or even without merit in providing financial services. Whether we are talking about insurance salespeople, brokers, or investment advisors, I am overall proud of the industry of financial professionals I belong to. While there may be a few bad apples in our profession, just like any business, I know from my interactions that the majority are great people who have the best intentions for their clients.

Yet, I have an issue with the overall preconceived notions about how to approach retirement planning and the common belief about what kind of outcome should be expected. The primary (and often only) goal I'm referring to is, "Don't outlive your savings."

Worse, the prevalent answer to this pre-established goal is to administer a remedy that is based upon a financial product. And this is where you'll find a division in the recommended product solution. Insurance salespeople are usually going to recommend "safe money" options like a guaranteed income solution with an annuity. Brokers will often offer mutual funds or a portfolio using asset allocation that is appropriate for their client's time horizon. Either will often refer to this simple income distribution plan as a retirement plan. It may be comprised of an OK insurance (annuity) product. It may even be a sound investment plan, but it falls far from a comprehensive financial plan. It's no wonder some retirees are misguided, as often these simplistic financial transactions are presented as a "financial plan." Often, these "plans" resemble a sales proposal. How can it be considered an actual plan when it does not address an individual's unique situation or the numerous variables that may impact future finances? Furthermore, as far as plans go, why would a plan be merely to sustain retirement?

Is this really the bar we're setting as an industry? Aren't we called to do more than just sell a product that, in the best-case scenario, ensures a couple doesn't outlive their savings? Shouldn't we set higher goals for the life's work and savings of our clients? Of course we should make sure people don't outlive their savings! But let's look beyond that! By focusing on a "secure retirement," we are missing so much more. I'm talking about opportunities for legacy planning as well as recognizing financial threats outside of standard' income distribution planning'. It seems that all too often, families and the advisors they pay to help them are playing to not lose instead of planning to win for their clients and their families. And this approach has led to a repeating cycle.

## THE REPEATING CYCLE

You might have heard the saying, "They made their money the old-fashioned way; they inherited it." But did you know that began as a humorous take from an 80's television commercial? Interestingly, it was an investment firm that had an actor end each plug with the statement, "They make their money the old-fashioned way; they earn it."

I grew up like most do, believing that the wealthy were an elite crowd lucky enough to be born that way. I never questioned how the family was well off in the first place or why their families would continue to be prosperous for generations. But I did understand all too well the path that most of us would take; starting with nothing and earning our own way in the world.

We make all the responsible moves, just like we're supposed to. We work hard in school so that we can get into a good college. We study in college and choose a career. We pour our heart and soul into a job for decades. Along the way, we sacrifice our time and save whatever we can. We endure life's ups and downs, personally and on the job. We continue to trudge along no matter what challenges we face. Along the way, we pay our taxes, try to help our kids with college, live within our means, build our 401Ks, and generally speaking, do everything right. And when the grind is finally finished, our reward is a retirement that we've funded.

To ensure we have enough to live out our years, we seek professional advice. A man in a suit and tie tells us we've done well for ourselves, and he'll ensure we don't run out of money before we die. Sure enough, most of us that have saved and invested wisely will accomplish just that. We probably have some good years before we end up in an assisted living facility.

And during this final phase of life, everything we've worked so hard for is reduced to a smidgen. After inflation, taxes, and healthcare costs, there is little if anything left for our loved ones. That's okay, we say, because our kids started from square one, just like us, and are doing fine. They'll be able to fund their own retirement. Meanwhile, your grandkids are starting from square one, hoping to build the same life we had—the cycle repeats.

# THE NOBLE CAUSE

I feel there is something noble and respectable for those that commit themselves to an education, a career, saving, and elevating their financial status. Most of my clients have built their wealth this way, and I've seen the results of their accomplishments. Many of them have made great sacrifices to provide a better way of life for their families. They have a great love for their spouses, children, and great causes they believe in. And yet, financial advisors settle for a comfortable retirement plan as the goal for the wealth they've accumulated.

Now, I've worked with people across all levels of economic means. I fully understand the value of assisting those with modest resources to make the best and enjoy as comfortable of a retirement as possible. It's true, sometimes a lack of savings doesn't allow or even justify much more than providing a little income to supplement social security.

But, multigenerational wealth planning isn't just for the super-wealthy! There's a misconception that financial planning beyond retirement is reserved for the uber-wealthy. The reality is that I work with everyday people to help them make the most of the assets they have. They aren't living in 10,000 square foot Hollywood mansions, driving Rolls Royces, or donating wings to colleges.

Their children and grandchildren probably won't be what you'd consider "trust fund babies." Yet, they do plan to protect their family from financial threats and wish to build a legacy. This often means they have plans to help future generations build on the foundation they've established.

*So, why don't most people insist upon financial goals beyond retirement?* I believe it comes down to two main reasons; they don't believe it's possible for them, or they don't know how.

## Actually, This Book Probably Is For You

Chances are, if you've picked up this book and read this far, your instincts are correct, and there's at least some guidance that can help you. Congratulations on taking a proactive approach to your finances and your family's well-being. I think this book will help clarify.

But some may have doubts and wonder if their assets are sufficient for the wealth management approach I'll be sharing. That's a valid concern. I understand not all retirees have a nest egg that justifies complex estate planning. I wish I could say there was a well-defined figure to distinguish who should pursue a financial legacy plan. But the reality is, it's very arbitrary. Starting on the low end of accumulated assets, I've had a few clients with under 6 figure savings that I've assisted with this process, primarily to protect the spouse. While it didn't require every aspect of the system, their particular situation's extenuating circumstances made it a good idea.

On the other end of the spectrum, those with a net worth over seven figures usually benefit from comprehensive financial planning, regardless of how close they are to retirement. Beyond just an investment plan, more assets require more extensive long-term tax planning. And of course, the reason behind this book, preserving wealth for the family should be a primary concern. I believe they will find great benefit from other financial management principles explained in this book, as well.

Outside of extenuating circumstance and a networth of over $1 Million, I often hesitate to do comprehensive planning for those who are years from retirement. While I may help with an investment plan, a complex financial plan likely isn't necessary at this point. However, such individuals will benefit from many of the lessons in this book. It will help them lay a foundation for a time when a professional advisor is necessary.

Personally, whom I choose to work with depends on many factors, aside from the size of their investment accounts.

With that said, I wrote this book for a specific target audience that I serve. Generally speaking, those with a total net worth (not just investable assets) that begin around $600,000 will find the most benefit in my lessons. Those who find themselves with a current estate value exceeding $2 million dollars will find particular value in my chapters addressing tax planning and estate transfer strategies and the information provided by Estate Planning Attorney Chad Ritchie. When applying the estate planning principles of this book, it's important to be cognizant that any current assets in the seven-figure range have the potential to face estate taxes. With years of portfolio growth, life insurance proceeds, real estate, on top of changing tax laws, more people than ever will need to plan for strategic wealth transfer.

But, it's not just about the size of the bank account; this is really for those concerned about the well-being of their spouse, children, and future generations. It's for those who want to have a plan in place for a time when they may not be here to guide and care for their loved ones physically. It's also for those who have causes that are dear to their heart and wish to make a difference. They are the legacy makers.

This book is for those who may already feel confident they have enough to preserve their lifestyle in retirement, even if they don't exactly know the best way to do so. They also have enough financial savvy to understand there are potential threats to their assets. There may be a calling to protect what they have earned, not just to preserve their own quality of life but also to better provide for those they may leave behind.

Often, they have questions regarding protection from taxes, long-term healthcare costs, inflation, market fluctuations, probate, surviving spouse's income sustainability, wealth transfer strategies, and more! They need a systematic approach to tie it all together for peace of mind.

I've found that it's when people are in the beginning stages of retirement or pre-retirement that they begin to concern themselves with long-range preparations. Therefore, the majority of the action steps will address those in the demographic of 55 and above. And yes, this includes people that have been successfully retired for years, as well.

But it's never too early to begin laying a foundation. I'm always impressed by those in their 30 and 40s who are anxious to pursue the financial planning process. I believe the content I provide in this book will be even more valuable to this age group than if I made my comprehensive financial planning service available to them.

## This Isn't For Everyone

On the other hand, this book isn't for everyone. Save yourself the time if you are convinced that just getting through retirement is the end goal. There are plenty of retirement planners all too happy to help meet that end. Or just as well, find a product on the internet that can offer a set income plan. Just one word of warning, an income solution based solely upon a product may be a risky venture.

Other than that, if you have no plans to have a family or causes you believe in, there's little reason to go through a process with the goal to leave a legacy.

Finally, for those with a net worth that exceeds ten million dollars in assets, I would suspect that you already understand the principles I've outlined in this book. My intention is to provide my readers the same level of financial education that the ultra-wealthy already apply to their finances.

I believe it's time that more of us applied a systematic approach to starting a new cycle of sustainable wealth for their families. The seven principles outlined in this book will help provide action steps towards generational wealth planning.

## A Special Bonus for Readers, from the Author!

Krista McBeath has recorded a video overview presentation of this book's contents!

Access this free workshop presentation at **www.McBeathFinancial.com/genwealth-seminar**

# CHAPTER TWO

# The Generational Wealth Wheel

D on't we all wish we could go back in time and coach ourselves? When I began in the financial services industry so many years ago, there was so much I didn't know. With my insurance background, it made sense to help people protect their retirement income with insurance products. To offer these insurance services as an independent agent, you must join a Field Marketing Organization (FMO).

FMO's serve agents nationwide in marketing, selling, and distributing insurance products. I learned early on that much of the training was about how to host paid dinner seminars. The point of offering a free steak was to convince people they needed to make an appointment to come and buy an annuity or a life insurance policy. They gave all the agents the same PowerPoint presentation, which had been used for years. In fact, you've probably noticed, it continues today. Granted, the emergence of coronavirus has mandated an adjustment; instead of postcard mailers for a "Free Steak Dinner Seminar," you'll see Facebook ads promoting webinars.

# THE RULES OF MONEY HAVE CHANGED

I've moved on, and my financial services practice has transformed. But looking back, I still remember the canned presentation topic, "The rules of money have changed." I would say that still rings true—more than ever. Not to rehash old news, but as a nation, the way we pay for our retirement has experienced an enormous shift. While previous generations had a defined benefit plan, aka pension, it's become almost universal that the risk of retirement now falls upon the back's of the employees.

Generations past would spend their entire career with one company. And that loyalty was rewarded with a nice pension that the employee could count on until the day they died. Somewhere along the way, major corporations decided they could control costs by shifting the responsibility of retirement to the employee. 401K plans gradually replaced pensions.

The changing times may be a cloud, but there's definitely a silver lining. While the masses could no longer count on their company benefits for their retirement, a whole new opportunity was created! People actually owned their retirement funds!

When companies stopped offering a pension, employees were no longer captive; They didn't have to remain with the same company their entire career to avoid losing their retirement. A new generation of a transient workforce was free to pursue opportunities at new companies with promotions and higher pay. And they were able to take their retirement with them! With the new 401K plans, they retained their retirement nest egg throughout the changes.

But before this significant shift, there was a time when retirement planning was relatively easy. In the old seminars, they referred to it as a three-legged stool consisting of social security, savings and pension. With the absence of pensions, it became a two-legged stool and the savings/

retirement account had to make up the difference.

'Retirement planners' jumped at the opportunity to capitalize on these assets now in the hands of the employees. They attempted to replicate a pension's retirement income with their own financial product. It was a quick and simple solution to the changing times.

Sure, income replacement products might be a suitable replacement to the pension – if that's all you were looking for. But my question is, why did it so often stop there!?! Too often, the greatest opportunity for generational wealth accumulation in history was being squandered due to shortcutting systems and strategy!

Yes, twenty years ago, we said the rules of money have changed. They are still changing and the playing field continues to evolve! Yet, why are so many in the financial services industry still offering the same solutions as they did twenty, thirty or more years ago? Why is the focus still upon either outperforming the market, or safe money? Shouldn't there have been an industry-wide evolution of how we help people manage their money?

With a different philosophy, money managers can implement a different strategy for wealth management. It's time for this generation to position themselves for a more secure retirement and in the process, *pass wealth on to the next generation.* I believe that's the most important obligation for any wealth management plan! While this is not the entirety of the wealth management process I'll be sharing, it's certainly the end goal.

# THE GENERATIONAL WEALTH WHEEL

I wish I could take full credit for creating every element of the Generational Wealth Wheel. The beauty is, so many great sources influenced the evolution of this system. It goes without saying I had an educational background in finance and insurance. I also have a foundation steeped in my various industry licenses as well as an advanced designation as a Chartered Financial Consultant. I read books, I attended educational seminars, there was financial technology software I learned and mastered, and endless research all along the way. I'm also very thankful for the influences of a few special industry mentors who encouraged financial planning over product sales.

I found ancillary skills were necessary to form a well-balanced financial plan. So in addition to investments and insurance, I developed a healthy background in taxes and estate planning. Tax planning began with years as a tax preparer. Estate planning benefitted from the close collaboration with Contributing Author attorney Chad Ritchie, a leader in field of Estate Planning.

While the individual pieces of the Wealth Wheel may not be unique, my systematic approach to integrating these essential pieces certainly is. The key ingredient for success isn't the various pieces of the puzzle but how they are arranged to work together.

I also believe a wealth management plan must be fully understood by the principle in order to function successfully. To that end, one of my key strengths has always been communication and collaboration. I've found that taking a seemingly complex undertaking and simplifying it to the essential easy action steps is critical to putting plans in motion.

# A HOLISTIC APPROACH TO WEALTH MANAGEMENT

A holistic approach to wealth management is essential for the preservation of lifestyle and legacy building. My wealth management process is comprised of six distinct intertwined financial aspects, along with an over encompassing tax strategy. To illustrate the concept, you'll notice the six-spoked captain's wheel below.

A ship captain's wheel is the perfect icon for the concepts I'll be explaining. Although some of the reasoning for a captain's wheel may be obvious, there's one very personal reason that most readers would never guess.

For starters, you might have already surmised that a ship wheel is excellent for analogies. *Of course,* I want to encourage you to grab the wheel and take control of your destiny! This whole book is about navigating your finances and adjusting along the way to meet your objectives, much like captaining a ship!

Second, I wanted to portray a circle. I am a huge Disney fan. I love the theme parks, the movies, the songs. So, it won't come as a surprise that I love the Disney classic, "The Lion King," featuring the song "The Circle of Life." I believe the show's theme of one generation passing on to the future generations in an endless circle to be very appropriate for the wealth management concepts I'm sharing.

Third, although the cycle of life may be viewed as a circle, planning for the phases of life isn't necessarily in a linear or chronological order. You'll notice that a captain's wheel is intersected by the six spokes that connect all the phases through a central hub. Likewise, I don't believe that each of the six steps are relegated to a defined time in one's life. More so, it's been my observation those who are conscientious of every aspect early in life will be the ones most prepared.

Furthermore, no single segment exists independently from the other five steps. When we look at holistic financial planning, we understand that each financial detail influences the overall unique situation. As such, no individual investment, transaction or financial strategy can exist in a bubble but must fit as part of the whole long-term plan to achieve goals.

The fourth reason why a ship's wheel is appropriate is the

perfect symmetry of the circle. This represents the balance necessary within an optimized plan. You'll notice every rung being equal and representing a distinct element of financial health. When the wheel is attached to these equal size rungs it forms a flawless circle. Such a design is necessary to captain a ship. Imagine a short spoke representing a financial aspect falling in neglect. Such a deficiency would lead to an imperfect circle and a defective captain's wheel. Just as a ship wouldn't steer easily with such a design, similarly, neglecting any aspect of one's financial health could severely hinder their ability to achieve financial goals.

## CAPTAIN NORM CLARK

Finally, I want to share a very personal reason why a captain's wheel is dear to my heart. A hero to me and one

of the most significant influences in my life was my father, nicknamed Captain Norm Clark. Yes, he was an air force veteran, and he was a pilot with his own small aviation company. But it was among family and close friends that he earned the moniker as 'Captain' from his years of piloting the family pontoon, the SS Minnow. His piloting skills of planes and boats were legendary, but his quiet leadership left the most significant impact on me. Some of my fondest family memories are from times we spent together boating on lakes. At the time, I didn't realize I was getting lessons in life, character, and morals, but I did. He left a legacy that was much more valuable than money.

I picture my dad's strong arm on that captain's wheel, confidently steering the boat, just as he helped guide me in my childhood. This memory serves as a personal reminder about what's truly important in life and why we manage our finances. At the root of all the financial strategies and tasks is one thing: The love for the people and causes we care about most.

## THE SIX SPOKES OF THE GENERATIONAL WEALTH WHEEL

I consider these indispensable principles of wealth management to be vital towards establishing multigenerational wealth.

# 1 Wealth Anchors

Basic financial principles are the building blocks for generational wealth. These common-sense guidelines are timeless and essential for accumulating and conserving wealth.

# 2 Income Streams

At least one source of cash flow will always be necessary to meet your family's monthly expenses. It's essential to plan for sustainable resources in the event of unemployment, disability, or the loss of a spouse. In retirement, a plan needs to include the impacts of market fluctuations, inflation and withdrawal rates.

# 3 Safety Nets

Minimize exposure to potential losses that can derail financial stability. Just as it's a foregone conclusion to insure assets such as a home, less obvious risks should be managed. Establish a plan to protect against potentially catastrophic threats to health, income, and investments.

# 4 Bold Growth

With the other principles engaged, investors can be at peace with pursuing asset growth. More aggressive wealth-building strategies can be employed when the stress of basic monetary needs and threats to the family's welfare is eliminated.

## 5 Celebrate Abundance

Our dreams are worth achieving! Enjoying the fruits of labor should be part of the financial plan. For those with a generous heart, advanced financial strategies can include the advantages of giving while living.

## 6 Charted Legacy

Protecting wishes and loved ones with legal and financial counsel is critical when it comes to transferring an estate. But it's more than financial assets that contribute to a lasting legacy for the next generation.

## Tax Strategy: The Hub of the Generational Wealth Wheel

Taxation over-encompasses all six spokes in some way or another. In many ways, a holistic tax strategy is what unites all the financial aspects. Tax strategies often weigh immediate tax reduction against long-term tax liabilities.

# THE VOYAGE

Instituting these seven wealth principles is only the beginning of ensuring future generations' financial security. Unfortunately, these aren't merely tasks to be completed once, allowing endless future generations to reap the rewards. Even a modest dynasty that can withstand the test of time requires two crucial qualities: fluidity and cultivation.

It's important to realize after a financial trajectory is established, it must remain fluid. A plan must always be flexible to adapt to changing circumstances, needs, and outside influences. Market forces and changes in laws – particularly tax laws – can drastically alter the financial landscape. Regular adjustments to plans will most likely be necessary for them to perform as desired.

Finally, I believe the most worthwhile investment we can make is the time we invest in future generations. Through our love and the energy we commit to our children and grandchildren, we can instill in them the foundations for success. We must take advantage of these years we have together to teach them the values and principles that will serve them well in life. It's even more critical they learn and pass them along to future generations.

# CHAPTER THREE

# Wealth Anchors

I watched the entire story unfold before my very eyes when a man was dropped off in an unfamiliar city with only $100 to his name and 90 days to turn it into a $1,000,000 business! I don't believe in get-rich-quick schemes, and I certainly don't teach them. Still, I was captivated by this individual's attitude and determination to push himself to the limit towards his goal.

Want to know how he did it? I definitely recommend seeing it for yourself! It was a special reality tv show on the Discovery Channel called Undercover Billionaire. The cameras followed Billionaire Glenn Stearns as he went undercover as a regular person. From the first episode, I was curious how he could possibly rise so fast without using his name, business connections, or even having a home! In an early episode, he actually was extremely sick, sleeping in his old truck, doing odd jobs, and even working a soup kitchen just so he could eat! What was inspiring was how his sacrifices, core values, and beliefs carried him from poverty to nearly a million-dollar business in less than three months!

The truth is, he didn't build that business in just three months. He had a lifetime of obstacles that prepared him for the challenge. At 56 years old, he had overcome growing up in poverty and a learning disability that led to him failing 4th grade. When he became a father at just 14 years old, he was forced to grow up fast. He worked hard, took advantage of every opportunity he could, and developed a mindset that eventually led him to great affluence as an owner of a lending company. After battling throat cancer and winning, some might say it was a mid-life crisis that sent him pursuing this challenge. Based on what I've seen, he wanted to prove something. The principles he learned through a lifetime of overcoming obstacles could work for anyone. The foundational beliefs he relied on took decades to build.

On the other end of the spectrum is an actress whose father was worth 500 million dollars at the time of his death. As a huge fan of the television series Beverly Hills 90210, I knew all the plot lines of Tori Spelling's character, Donna Martin. I also knew that her dad was somehow connected in Hollywood. It turns out he was quite influential and wealthy, and Tori grew up in a life of privilege. Unfortunately, she failed to learn basic financial self-restraint. While her father was extremely wealthy, he failed to educate her and instill wisdom when it came to money. Realizing her spendthrift ways were her detriment, upon his passing, he left her a mere $800,000 after taxes, which didn't last long. After unpaid debts of hundreds of thousands to banks, American Express, and tax liens, she's relied upon her mom to cover basic living expenses.

She's even admitted her issues, quoted as saying "It's no mystery why I have money problems. I grew up rich beyond anyone's dreams. Even when I try to embrace a simpler lifestyle, I can't seem to let go of my expensive tastes."

## What Separates the Two Stories?

I marvel at the contrast in these two stories. I ask myself if Glenn Stearns learned a secret to wealth that Aaron Spelling failed to teach his daughter. If we knew what separated the two, wouldn't we want to know it as we're trying to improve our own financial position? More importantly, wouldn't we want to share it with our children?

The problem is, for many of those that have accrued financial success, it's taken a lifetime of sacrifice, saving, and doing all of the 'right things'. Over time, the attitudes, habits, and work ethic that made success possible have become unconscious traits that they take for granted. To exacerbate the problem, the children have also grown up accustomed to the *results* of the traits that brought success. So, it's no wonder that there may be a challenge in teaching the next generation, especially when it's hard to pinpoint exactly what led to the accumulated wealth.

Experts will agree that it's essential to talk to our children about money. Usually, they recommend simple talking points. How many times have we heard that you should start teaching your young kids about money with an allowance and maybe even starting a savings account? Then, jump ahead forty years; we're supposed to have a conversation with our adult children about our financial situation and what to expect. Hmmm, it seems like there might be something missing here, doesn't it? Could this be the reason why statistically, wealth seldom lasts past the third generation?

So, what do our children need to understand and pass on to their own children? Let's start with the basics.

# THE BASICS

There may be many different factors that lead to financial success, but I believe at a simple level, it comes down to two main ingredients: mindset and basic accounting (cashflow) principles. Put another way, having the wisdom to make sound financial decisions on a regular basis. Some might call this common sense.

You've also probably noticed that common sense isn't all that common these days. A well-known radio talk show host has even made a multi-million dollar career from dispensing the most basic financial advice to the masses. If one is starting out and looking for a basic education, Financial Peace classes aren't a bad place to look. One word of caution, I think radio show experts sometimes over-extend their expertise when it comes to advice beyond young families or novices to money management. Without a thorough understanding of the individual's financial picture, sweeping recommendations are questionable for more mature investors. This is even more true when the 'expert' has no relevant education or credentials in the field he's dispensing advice.

Dave Ramsey is just one of many financial gurus that cover the essentials. There are many, many books that do an excellent job of deep-diving into the basics of personal finance. This book isn't intended to be one of them.

Since most people reading this will have advanced beyond the beginner level, I'll simply offer the essentials that must be passed on for perpetual wealth through the next generation and beyond.

# SEESAW OF MONEY

Accounting is a critical part of every business. At a simple level, its function is tracking the company's financial position and using that data to guide prudent business decisions. While most people don't actually own a business, it might be wise to adopt a business owner's mindset when it comes to their personal finances. Think of it as You Incorporated! Each of us is responsible for our own personal financial situation. As such, we need to treat it like our own business, regardless of the source of our income.

The great news is, it doesn't have to be complex, and you don't have to be able to run advanced accounting reports. In fact, without running spreadsheets and reports, I'm going to share an easy-to-learn (and teach) principle for increasing wealth through cash flow management.

We all know we should spend less than we make, right? Otherwise, we might find we have too much month left at the end of our money! But do we really understand the cumulative value of the little decisions we make towards 'living within our means' and how it impacts our wealth over the long term?

To illustrate these concepts, picture a seesaw with an arrow representing where the weight is, representing the current financial position. The very center point would represent equilibrium, where the seesaw is perfectly balanced and horizontal to the ground.

**Figure 1.1 Balance**

This position would represent where all monthly expenses equal all monthly income. It's definitely a difficult balancing act, and it's often referred to as living pay-check to pay-check.

Now, picture what happens in this scenario when the unexpected happens. It could be a health issue, unexpected unemployment, or even a major car repair.

Whatever the case may be, suddenly, the arrow has shifted slightly to the right, representing a monthly deficit.

**Figure 1.2 Deficit**

Without reserves or other sources of income to make up the shortfall, the deficit is covered by debt. In most households, credit cards are used. In addition to the debt itself, the cost to service the debt is now an additional expense. This additional expense further moves the arrow to the right and moves finances further out of balance, a little more every month.

**Figure 1.3 Deficit in Motion**

Running at a monthly deficit causes a variety of additional expenses, which compound the problem. In addition to paying interest, such a deficit often means paying bills late with late charges and slipping credit scores. This leads to higher interest rates for mortgages and higher car insurance premiums, only making the slide worse. And usually, additional debt is added to make ends meet. This is why it's said the poor get poorer.

Remember George Foreman, former boxing heavy-weight champion, pitching his grill? Think of the debt as George Foreman, sitting on the deficit side of that seesaw. The longer he sits there, the more cheeseburgers he eats and the heavier he gets. You know it's only a matter of time until his end of the seesaw collapses to the ground. Similarly, in the worst-case scenario, when the weight of the right side of the seesaw is overwhelmed with debt, it hits the ground. Bankruptcy.

**Figure 1.4 Bankruptcy**

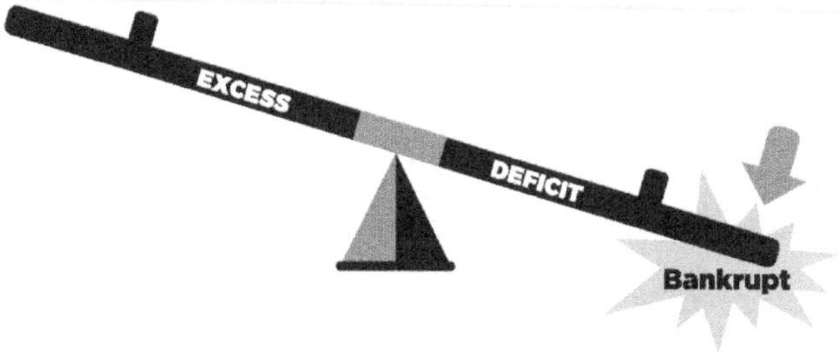

Fortunately, in most cases, bankruptcy is avoided. A sudden cash infusion, such as a gift, a bonus, or possibly even a tax return, may help balance the scales. Other times, people might reverse the trend by either increasing their monthly income or reducing their monthly expenditures.

Continuing further to the left, when income outpaces spending, the arrow moves past the 'tipping point'. This is where the principles of money management begin to work on behalf of people.

**Figure 1.5 Excess**

Without any further changes to income or expenses, dynamic principles will start happening that continue to move the arrow further along to the left. Bills can be paid on time, improving credit. You can expect favorable mortgage rates and lower car insurance rates. Instead of paying interest on credit cards, you can pay them off at the end of the month, and the credit card companies *are paying you with cash back!* Furthermore, the excess can be saved and invested, creating additional resources. This is just another reason the rich get richer, as the saying goes.

Over years of applying these principles, eventually, all

debt, including the mortgage, is paid off, reducing expenses further. Meanwhile, investments have the potential of becoming income-producing assets. This passive income may result from rental property, annuities, stock dividends, or any other cash flow produced as a result of investments.

When the income from these investments is enough to cover monthly expenses, without drawing from the principle, it is considered financially independent. It has the potential of generating perpetual income, independent of earned wages from employment.

Figure 1.6 Financial Independence

If this income source is reliable, theoretically, one could safely retire regardless of age, without fear of outliving their money. In such a scenario, it's extremely important to calculate all the risks and plan carefully for a more secure extended retirement period. Market fluctuations, inflation, taxes, healthcare costs, and other factors could potentially necessitate a drawdown of the principle.

Of course, you can retire before attaining this, and most do.

Figure 1.7 Income With Earned Wages

But to meet monthly expenses without employment wages, you'll most likely be drawing into your principle and could risk depleting your retirement funds. It's critical to have a strong financial plan that includes solid income planning and risk analysis at this point. The illustration below shows that by retiring at this point, there is an income deficit. Achieving balance can only be bridged by cutting expenses, accessing the capital from investments, part-time work income and/or social security.

Figure 1.8 Income Without Earned Wages

Some do achieve the enviable position of wealth beyond financial independence. They reach a point where their wealth continues to grow, without earned income. There is little risk of outliving their assets. In this position, tax and estate planning are important for the strategic transfer of wealth.

**Figure 1.9 Abundant Wealth**

Not everyone is going to achieve that level of extreme wealth, but I believe everybody that works towards it and plans deserves a comfortable retirement. I also feel it's important to have something to leave behind as a legacy of your life's sacrifices. The best way to do that is to work towards moving your arrow as far left as possible, with the goal of achieving and surpassing the financially independent mark, as illustrated in Figure 1.6.

# BUDGETING

Budgeting is an over-used term that makes most people cringe at the thought. The very words 'set up a budget' makes it sound like I'm reigning in the freedom to choose how money is spent. So let me be clear, the purpose of a budget is to achieve financial freedom! If it works towards achieving that, it's not even necessary for it to be ultra-strict or defined. It can be as simple as a goal not to exceed spending a certain amount of money every month and sticking to it! It can be more detailed, only if you find it necessary.

Essentially budgeting is all about taking control of your finances. Part of this is understanding where your income is going and aligning that with your budgetary goals. It's not about taking away your simple pleasures, such as your Starbucks double chocolate chip frappe or even a nice dinner out with the family. Sure, the little things can add up, but the big things count even more. I don't know anyone that went broke from buying coffee, but I've seen many people buried in credit card debt from purchasing things they didn't need. The big things count. Boats, luxury vehicles, swimming pools, timeshares, kitchen remodels *can all be great purchases at the right time when they fit within a planned budget!*

This all seems obvious, but here's something that isn't so obvious and I feel is even more hazardous to your financial foundation. The little monthly recurring expenses. We live in an age where there are more temptations than ever before to add so many small expenses that happen month after month! I'll go on the record to say I consider a cell phone and home internet service as essentials. Beyond that are entertainment services like cable tv, Netflix, Hulu, Disney+, Sling, Apple TV, Amazon and Apple music, Spotify, and dozens of other subscription services available for our phone apps.

Most of these expenses seem small, but they add up, and since they are automatically deducted from an account monthly, they are easy to miss. Are there other monthly expenses we are choosing to ignore? You bet! How about gym memberships, the appliances or furniture we bought on a monthly payment plan, or even a car payment! Together, these all can add up to an overwhelming burden. And we have a whole new generation that has been indoctrinated to accept these monthly charges without questioning if they are even necessary! Many of these recurring charges are luxuries that can act as wealth leaches.

Since income usually remains steady every month, these recurring expenses should be monitored and limited where possible. And of course, a budget to track cash outflow is the best way to manage these leaks.

My father-in-law still uses a complex handwritten spreadsheet for his budgeting and measures every bill down to the penny by hand! He has some accounting background from the early 70's and never migrated when advanced technology became available. Thankfully, we have now have tools at our disposal that make the process of tracking income and expenses a breeze!

## WEALTH MANAGEMENT TOOLS

As a financial planner, I utilize an easy – and secure – tracking system that automates this process. It allows for the linking of personal accounts for automated tracking of the incoming and outgoing cash flow. Our suite of Wealth Management Tools allows our clients to stay connected to their entire financial picture. All their essential financial information is accessible in one place, updated in real-time for secure online access at their fingertips.

These Wealth Management Tools are an essential part of our Technology Empowered Advisor Method (TEAM) approach to financial planning. The advanced cash flow mapping features are critical as people enter retirement. I utilize it as part of my advanced comprehensive financial planning program.

The automated tracking features are great to help individuals of all ages that wish to track financial goals! As a special bonus to my readers, I'm offering complimentary access to our software. This Personal Wealth Management Website will allow you to easily manage incoming and outgoing expenses and much more. You can learn more and register at www.mcbeathfinancial.com/wealth-management-tools-registration/

## BEGINNER'S WEALTH TASK LIST

Getting your expenses and income to balance is an excellent primary goal. But we all know how hard it is; we hope there is excess at the end of the month for savings when starting out. It takes discipline, for sure, but also having automated systems in place can help.

I also agree with many of the basics for wealth building. Rather than go into great detail on information readily available elsewhere, I'm including a quick checklist.

- ✓ Contribute to your employer's 401k up to the maximum amount they match.
- ✓ Pay off high-interest credit card debts.
- ✓ Establish an emergency fund equal to 6 months of living expenses.
- ✓ Protect your family with term life insurance.
- ✓ Purchase a reasonably priced home. You should

NOT spend as much as the mortgage lender allows. Keep the mortgage costs under 25% of after-tax income.

✓ Contribute the maximum to a Roth IRA based on eligibility.

Beyond these basics, I would also recommend establishing is a monthly automatic ACH withdrawal from your checking to go to a savings account. Set this withdrawal for 10% of your paycheck, coinciding with the date you get paid. The philosophy is, you are paying yourself first! Have the mindset that your earned money is like any other bill that needs to be paid every month – to yourself! This can be the basis of the emergency account and eventually it can go towards investments above your 401k. If you wait to save what's left at the end of the month, instead of withdrawing the savings first, you'll find much less available.

These are simple tasks that will help build a foundation and is by no means an inclusive list. But following basic principles in most cases will lead to a growth in assets.

At a certain point, more complex financial strategies will be of benefit. I recommend that someone over 55 or those with over $250,000 in investible assets (outside a current employer's 401K) to seek professional counsel. Mistakes at this point are elevated in potential damage. Also, professional advisors may be advantageous in identifying opportunities for your unique financial situation.

# MINDSET FOR WEALTH

The principles of the foundation are, first and foremost, a mindset. Without the proper beliefs and values, the rest of the wealth-building principles will fail. It's of particular importance that parents who are undertaking Legacy Planning impart these values upon the next generation.

Two polar opposite mentalities can interfere with creating, keeping, and passing wealth on to the next generation. It's the spender's mentality vs. the saver's mentality; each of these can be detrimental at the wrong time and place.

Let's cover the obvious, which is the spendthrift. Habits that favor instant gratification and finding joy in material objects can lead to debt. Over time, this is adverse to building wealth and its preservation, agreed? A certain amount of discipline is required to steward finances in a manner that preserves wealth. Honestly, I seldom encounter people with these traits in my professional business for obvious reasons.

What I do encounter regularly are those who have done an excellent job of sacrificing and reigning in expenses over the course of their lifetime. In addition to building a large nest egg, they've also done an excellent job of educating themselves in money along the way. It's these traits that have allowed them to amass a tidy sum. Unfortunately, these very attitudes can also handicap some people as they get near the finish line of retirement.

Specifically, I'm referring to the reluctance to hire and follow paid professionals' advice regarding money matters. Some prefer a do-it-yourself approach, while others feel the professional fees are too expensive.

I can appreciate those with a DIY mentality, and I applaud their dedication and attention to their finances. However, there comes the point where it's advantageous to bring in third-party professionals to the table when wishing to take finances to the next stage. Financial advisors, accountants, and attorneys can often offer critical insights and guidance and potentially serve as a transition team. Financially and emotionally, it leaves survivors much better equipped when the inevitable happens.

I'll also concede that great financial professionals can be expensive. They are costly for many well-justified reasons and worth it. But rather than justify the fees charged, the real question is, *do they bring more value to your finances than they cost?* If they are critical to achieving the financial goals, then probably. Additionally, if the fees are less than the added return they provide, or losses they circumvent, *don't the professional fees pay for themselves?*

CHAPTER FOUR

# Income Streams

The year was 1993, and Stanley Kirk Burrell was living life on top of the world. He was jet-setting around the world in private planes with a 200 person entourage he was paying $500,000 every month. The twenty-million-dollar home he had custom-built included a twenty-car garage filled with high-end luxury cars. It even had a real gold toilet! With a rapid rise to fame, he had earned over forty-nine million dollars in just three years!

And yet, just three years later, he managed to amass so much debt that he was forced into bankruptcy.

As the rapper sensation of the early 90s, everyone knew his name…MC Hammer! Remember, he sang, "U can't touch this." It turns out the IRS proved him wrong. After his unsustainable lifestyle came crashing down, he was saddled with numerous tax liens that remained a liability for years.

Conversely, somewhere in the hot south, there's a guy in his late 60s sitting on several hundred thousand dollars in a bank savings account. He's living in a mobile home with no air conditioning, wearing the same sweat-stained pair of underwear he's owned for ten years. Living on spam, crackers and Hamm's Beer, he wouldn't dream of touching his savings out of fear of going broke! No, not a former celebrity this time, but a vivid illustration of someone living far below their means for absolutely no good reason!

Notice the stark contrast in the consequences of living a lifestyle outside of one's means. While exaggerated, it's actually quite common to find retirees facing a crisis from either spending recklessly or, just as bad, failing to enjoy the life they could! The key is finding a happy medium in a sustainable lifestyle that fit's nicely within the resources available. It's possible to enjoy the best life possible without the fear of impending financial ruin! It's the sweet spot between excess and needless sacrifice found by budgeting and planning towards personal goals.

While this is a part of what I do within every financial

plan, one particular couple comes to mind as living their retirement dreams. They both will soon retire before the age of 60 from their corporate jobs with respectable retirement accounts, giving them freedom at a relatively young age. Their dream wasn't for a mansion or expensive sports cars, but they wanted what brings them the most happiness. Together, we've put together a life plan that allows them to do what they most enjoy: Travel!

They share so much happiness together while traveling the world! They'd just gotten back from the Caribbean, and then I called them the next week, and they were at Disney. They have plotted a sustainable lifestyle plan that includes a very healthy vacation budget! Yes, they are well off, but I wouldn't consider them the ultra-wealthy you read about in magazines. They merely worked hard, saved, and planned the distribution of their assets in a manner that protected their lifestyle priorities throughout their expected lifespan.

## RETIREMENT SIMPLIFIED

The actual act of retiring often feels like a terrifying prospect, regardless of assets. After years of receiving regular paychecks, suddenly, they stop. Many feel like they are now walking a high-wire without a safety net.

In initial meetings, prospective clients often ask if they *can* retire. Well, without even looking at their retirement accounts, I can quickly answer that question. It would be, "Yes, you can retire, of course. Masses of people with absolutely no retirement savings retire every day." However, those people are not likely retiring successfully, and that's not answering the real questions: Are their income sources and savings accounts enough to maintain their lifestyle? Can they maintain the standard of living they want without fear of depleting their resources within their lifetime? Do they have to worry about a surviving spouse if one of them passes away? And those interested in legacy planning want to know how much they'll be able to pass on to their heirs.

Finding the answer to their question does require delving into more of the particulars of their situation. On a basic level, it comes down to calculating monthly expenses and taxes, and then creating an income plan to cover those expenses.

So, the first step is adding up all of the monthly household expenses. Although this may not be too much of a challenge, it is much more complex when estimating the expenses 10, 20, or 30 years down the road. Inflation, increased medical costs, tax changes, and other variables must be accounted for.

Next, calculate the total pensions, social security, and any other guaranteed income sources. If these fall short of covering monthly expenses, creating a distribution plan from retirement accounts or other investments to cover the shortfall will be necessary.

While this may seem relatively simple, calculations are extremely detailed in accounting for numerous variables when extrapolating such data over a long period of time. At the most superficial level, you'll need to account for market fluctuations in the portfolio as well as the growth rate! Pursuing too much growth can risk retirement security, while an inadequate rate of return could lead to exhausting retirement accounts too soon.

A highly skilled comprehensive financial planner will utilize a specific suite of advanced software tools to provide projections and strategies. They are indispensable when building a sizable financial picture showing the year-by-year forecasts. Detailed cash flow illustrations can portray calculations based on income, expenses, inflation, liabilities, taxes, and more.

# TRANSFORMING ASSETS INTO CASHFLOW

When that last paycheck is deposited and spent, it can be somewhat unsettling to realize it's the last earned income. Suddenly it may be necessary to rely on retirement accounts to help cover living expenses.

At this point, most people have been diligently saving for decades, accumulating 'untouchable' retirement accounts. And the day comes where the vault doors are thrown wide open, and the amassed sum is sitting there just waiting to be spent! It's what they've prepared for, yet having this large sum of money at the fingertips often causes anxiety about the best way to use it.

Obviously, it wouldn't be wisest to treat retirement accounts like an ATM cash dispenser and spend the savings however and whenever wanted. With the realization that retirement funds are a finite resource, it's probably a good idea to develop a plan to position them for a sustainable income.

What if you had an overall strategy that would allow you to feel confident and will help provide for you and your family throughout this stage of your life? A solid financial plan will be your guide for accessing retirement savings to provide reliable monthly income.

A vital element of every distribution plan is assessing the post-retirement cash flow needs. It's a widely accepted rule of thumb that retirees can get by with 70% of their pre-retirement income. However, it's my experience most recent retirees are busy and want to enjoy the life they've earned. I feel a better starting point is to expect the same monthly expenses as before retirement. But, long-term planning could reveal an income deficit or a low probability of financial success, meaning you risk running out of money at such spending levels. In such cases, it may be necessary to address the budget and adjust the plan.

Once a monthly budget is established, assess available income sources to cover the monthly expenses. About 30% of Americans still have pension income, which is taken into account first. Some have other sources of income, such as a spouse's wage income, farm rents, property rentals, etc.

Social Security will also supplement income, but it only covers about 33 percent of a retiree's basic needs for most people. Advanced software can help calculate the best overall strategy for claiming social security benefits when building a comprehensive financial plan. To advise on the optimal age for filing, a holistic plan must include considerations for income, investments, expenses, Medicare premiums and surcharges, and tax strategy.

After adding up pensions, Social Security, and any other income sources, subtract the projected monthly expenditures and taxes to reveal any budget gaps. When there's a deficiency, distributions from retirement accounts come into play to make up the difference.

# WITHDRAWAL STRATEGIES

There are many ways to convert retirement accounts into a regular income stream to provide for living expenses. Which investment vehicle is used depends on the individual's needs. We often create a plan that utilizes more than one vehicle to achieve the goals; I like to call this bucket planning. Building an income plan is a balancing act based upon immediate, short-term, and long-term needs. The more immediate needs are, the more conservative our approach likely is. Assets that will be used for future income can then focus on growth. Because we have to consider inflation, taxes, market fluctuations, potential long-term healthcare, changes to income after a spouse passes away, and other unknowns, it's important to choose the right balance of financial vehicles.

In most cases, the bulk of your retirement savings will be in an IRA or 401k, which can be withdrawn from on a regular basis, subject to some rules. Typically most employer retirement accounts will have a mixture of equities and fixed income options that align with risk tolerance or growth goals. These stocks and bonds are usually held within the mutual fund choices offered by the employer's retirement plan. My recommendations are usually to use Exchange Traded Funds (ETF's), instead of Mutual Funds, if you have the option. ETFs offer the diversity of mutual funds, but normally have lower fees and are more tax-efficient in after-tax accounts.

Once in a while, I'll offset some of the risks of market-based investments with insurance-based vehicles, such as Fixed Indexed Annuities (FIA). I prefer the use of FIA's over Variable Annuities because of the risk and high fees typically associated with Variable Annuities. FIA's can help hedge against the stock market's volatility and can provide for a guaranteed income stream. Once your predictable income plan is in place, you might feel more comfortable focusing on a growth strategy with the remainder of your portfolio assets.

Lastly, I'll mention an Indexed Universal Life Policy as a source of retirement income. I feel this product can be particularly advantageous for high net worth individuals as part of an overall retirement and tax strategy. Since the product's cash value is most often tied to an external index, such as the S&P 500, it can also have strong growth potential. While many may scoff at the use of a life insurance policy for tax-advantaged income and wealth transfer, the projections from illustrations speak for themselves. Dismissing such a strategy solely because it's a product classified under the insurance umbrella could be a costly oversight in both growth and tax savings.

# WITHDRAWAL RATE

There's a psychological leap between experiencing market fluctuations in a retirement account while still contributing and working compared to watching the balance drop while actively taking disbursements during retirement. While an income plan built around guaranteed withdrawals from annuities and pensions may not have depletions risks, it's crucial to control the withdrawal rate when deriving income from market-based accounts. Market drops and large distributions earlier in retirement could particularly affect plans dependent upon portfolio growth.

One widely accepted principle is the 4% rule, which states

that you can safely withdraw 4% of the asset's principal every year without the risk of running out of money in retirement. Considering the S&P 500 has returned an average annual rate of about 11% over the last 30 years, a heavily weighted equities portfolio most likely wouldn't touch the principle.

However, I don't adhere to the 4% rule as a good plan for a withdrawal strategy. Here's what could happen by relying on this surefire '4%' rule: First, historical averages do not guarantee future results. There are no guarantees in the equity markets. Furthermore, the ups and downs of the market from year to year can cause a *sequence of returns risk*, lowering individual returns. Finally, a 4% withdrawal may provide insufficient funds for the lifestyle they desire for some people.

So what happens if you need more than a 4% distribution to cover the gap between your income and expenses? In many cases, calculations at a 7% withdrawal still project high rates of success. However, if there are limited retirement funds available, coupled with longevity, the real risk is outliving your money. Does it now make sense to pursue a higher return? Maybe, but that doesn't come without risks. Either way, retirement planning software should be used to stress-test the likely success rate of either plan, weighing longevity risks, inflation, and market fluctuations.

However, those pursuing a generational wealth strategy are most likely not facing the risk of running out of funds in retirement. Most seeking estate planning strategies have more than sufficient assets to fund their chosen retirement lifestyle endlessly. In such cases, a 4% withdrawal rate would have two major flaws. First, for large retirement accounts, withdrawing excess funds beyond what's necessary would create tax liabilities. Furthermore, you might sacrifice growth on the money that is earmarked for withdrawal if it is not reinvested, which by the way, will typically create more taxes!

# FORCED WITHDRAWALS

Many retirees haven't planned for the tax time-bomb of forced retirement account withdrawals that exceed their living expenses. Upon reaching 72, regular withdrawals are required from 401(K)s, IRAs, and other similar qualified retirement accounts. Since the contributions to those accounts were not previously taxed, the Required Minimum Distributions (RMDs) are taxable when disbursed.

While working, the tax savings offered by retirement

accounts was beneficial. The widely believed assumption is that in retirement, income will be much lower; thus it's better to pay the taxes at the time of distribution because taxes will be lower. However, after decades of substantial savings and growth, many retirees find the RMDs are creating a much bigger tax problem than anticipated. They may actually reach a point of being forced into a *higher tax bracket in retirement!*

The truth is, many retirees are blindsided by the taxes they end up paying in retirement. As their regular RMDs are distributed, many pay all the taxes and deposit the remainder in investment accounts. Maybe they are gifting some of the money that's left after taxes to their family. Or, perhaps they're turning around and investing the remainder of the forced withdrawals. These taxed investments can create even more future tax for themselves and, very likely, their children. Capital gains taxes, income taxes, and estate taxes may be incurred! *In addition, the Biden administration is talking about getting rid of the stepped-up cost basis, which means all of their investment accounts that they have right now are just going to create more taxes!*

And in the meantime, their IRAs are creating this total tax time-bomb for their heirs. Let's say by the time a son or a daughter inherits a mature IRA, it's worth well over three million dollars. With ten years to take these distributions, he/she is likely facing an extra three hundred thousand dollars a year in taxable income! For starters, this would probably push their child in an incredibly high tax bracket, based upon him likely being in his peak earning years at the time. It will also very likely cause increased premiums on his Medicare, if age 65+, as well as a surtax on his investment income. This distribution avalanche could cause a ripple effect to his overall tax burden beyond standard income tax. Multiple points of taxation can have a dramatic impact on the legacy left behind. And it's all completely avoidable.

A financial planner with tax planning expertise and the proper software tools can help look forward to see if such an event is likely. With foresight, some strategies may help avoid such a pitfall. Roth IRA conversions or other tax strategies are but a few I'll be covering in this book.

# EXCESS INCOME

In such cases where excess income is causing rampant tax liabilities, life insurance can be an excellent tool for passing along wealth to future generations. Unfortunately, the cost component of life insurance can cause many to overlook the long-term financial benefits for the family. I understand why they may feel as if life insurance isn't necessary, but it's often the most effective solution for the problem, with incredible advantages.

Here's a typical example of a couple in their mid-seventies with close to two million dollars in their IRA. As you can imagine, RMD withdrawals are substantial, and the amount of taxes paid are disconcerting. I often find myself trying to explain that there's no way to completely avoid paying taxes on RMDS from an IRA unless they are willing to part with that money.

What do I mean? A Qualified Charitable Distribution (QCD) can help minimize or mitigate that tax with a calculated disbursement to a charitable organization. It's an excellent strategy for wealth transfer, I'll explain in chapter 11. But often, what I see is retirees using their excess income to gift significant amounts of money to their families. I understand; it's a great feeling to help kids with a home purchase or maybe help a grandchild with college expenses. Gratifying, but what happens with excess funds beyond their families' immediate needs?

I'll point out that they're not going to spend all of their excess money, and ultimately, it's going to pass to their son and their grandchild anyway. So instead of gifting a sum of fifteen thousand annually, why not start using those more significant dollar amounts that are causing them taxes regardless and putting that into something more meaningful for their family?

Perhaps certain older clients won't qualify for life insurance, but they could undoubtedly buy and pay for a life insurance policy on their children's lives and even their children's spouses if they wanted to. So in exchange for some premium with dollars that are already taxed, they can provide a tax-free death benefit to an heir if something happens to their child. That might not be their top concern, but it's still pretty powerful. Also, from a tax standpoint, they are still paying the same taxes on the income they were before, but they are able to provide a much greater benefit for the children and grandchildren!

The second thing that it would allow the grown child to do is to be able to pull out of this life insurance policy on a tax-free basis in retirement, using the cash value to create a tax-free income for himself. It's a powerful way to turn a tax liability into a legacy!

Whenever too much retirement income is a significant issue because of the accompanying tax liability, it's wise to lower the overall tax liability and create an estate plan that allows more assets to pass on to the next generation or a charity. Long-term tax planning requires looking at the big picture and not the upfront cost.

# SEQUENCE FOR ACCESSING ACCOUNTS

Establishing a plan for taking withdrawals is an integral part of the strategy, often with multiple accounts set up to access during different phases of retirement. Which account to draw from first depends on the individual's financial situation. For example, for some, taking social security at 62 makes the most sense, and for others, delaying until full retirement age or 70 is better. Sometimes, spending down the retirement accounts first provides the greatest overall tax savings.

The truth is, there's no one 'perfect' strategy that can meet the needs of everyone. Usually, spouses are of different ages with different retirement dates, each holding various 401ks and other investments. It's a precise balancing act to provide a path for the best strategy suited for them. Without a proper plan, there may be tax implications, unwarranted risk, and hindered growth factors resulting from tapping the wrong investment accounts.

# PRIORITIZE SOLUTIONS OVER PRODUCTS

A fiduciary is a financial advisor bound to putting their clients' interests first. That means they are required to focus on providing the best solution possible, which isn't based on selling a particular financial product. Non-fiduciaries only requirement is to sell a product that will be suitable for their customer's needs, *regardless of if it is the best solution* for the client. As a result, it's legal, if not ethical, to prioritize selling a product that offers an advisor or firm the greatest rewards. This may be why some 'in-house' branded mutual funds or insurance products are often viewed with skepticism. They may be fine products, but are they the *right product* for the individual's circumstances?

A successful income plan or estate plan is tailor-made for the individual first and foremost. It's critical to understand the customer's overall risk tolerance, goals, and feelings regarding their money. Other factors that will direct a cash flow plan include expected longevity, healthcare considerations, the importance of legacy planning, and surviving spouse income safeguards. Since each individual's situation is unique, the financial products used to build the income plans can vary significantly from person to person.

# THE IMPORTANCE OF PROFESSIONAL ASSISTANCE

For some, running out of money in retirement may not be a concern, but did you know there's another real risk many people face? *Failing to live their best life possible while securing their family's financial future!* One of the most important things a financial planner can provide is peace of mind. With all the years spent saving for retirement, doesn't it make sense to plan for how to spend it? Shouldn't that plan include the well-deserved personal rewards while still providing for loved ones?

A financial planner has experience and advanced software tools to create a customized plan. A good financial plan goes beyond retirement income. It ties in all the most critical financial considerations: access to emergency funds, tax strategies, probate avoidance, a legacy plan, and much more. The goal isn't just to skimp by but to bring you the joy, peace, and satisfaction to enjoy the retirement you've earned!

### References

1. https://www.celebritynetworth.com/richest-celebrities/richest-rappers/mc-hammer-net-worth/

2. https://www.fool.com/investing/how-to-invest/stocks/average-stock-market-return/

3. https://www.nerdwallet.com/investing/retirement-calculator

# CHAPTER FIVE

# Safety Nets

It's amazing how the entire course of a person's life can change in an instant. A singular unexpected event can send all our plans into a tailspin, and the ripples of such an event can send us down an entirely new path. I'll never forget the day where my life seemed to stop on a dime and the difficult after-effects that shaped my mission to help others.

I stepped out onto Illinois State University campus, relieved to have completed my last final of the year! As I breathed in the fresh spring air, I remember looking forward to a stress-free summer before my final year of college. I was exhausted and headed back to my sorority house to take a nap after being up most of the night studying. I remember the phone ringing, but I didn't bother to answer it. A few minutes later there was a knock on my door; my Grandmother was holding on our house phone line downstairs. I knew something was wrong and this call sent my world into a crisis.

She told me I had to come quickly; my dad had been admitted to the hospital with sudden heart complications. Bedside at the hospital, I learned he had barely avoided a massive heart attack. Throughout the following week, we prayed for his recovery as he remained in the ICU. He miraculously survived the event but did not come out unscathed. There was a long road to recovery, and health issues would continue to haunt him for the rest of his life.

Alone, the event was bad enough, but at a time when he needed peace, the financial stress was overwhelming. With a lengthy hospital stay and then the recovery, my parents faced the perfect storm of an endless sea of medical bills. Since they were self-employed, it meant the bills piled up at the very time their income was impacted the most. See, they were both self-employed, and unfortunately, this meant they were largely unprotected from such a crisis at that time. I witnessed firsthand the emotional and financial devastation because of inadequate insurance and financial preparation for this kind of unexpected life event.

Seeing the impact and aftermath led to my career passion for helping other families adequately prepare themselves to avoid financial worries and burdens. I felt I had a personal stake in completing my final year at ISU, and I earned my Bachelors Degree in Insurance to go along with my degree in Business Administration. I immediately thereafter began my career as an insurance agent with a dedication to protecting clients from catastrophic life events.

## WHY INSURANCE?

When I bring up insurance, the first instinct might be to roll your eyes and skip to the next chapter. *And that would be a huge mistake.* When used correctly, insurance can help you leverage resources to grow wealth and avoid risks that could be cataclysmic. Simply put, a relatively small amount of money can shift the burden of risk and unknowns onto the underwriting insurance company.

I just want to be very clear on something. I didn't pursue an insurance career to be a stereotypical pushy life insurance agent. Trust me, I laugh at the portrayal of those people as well. One of my favorites is the life insurance salesman Ned Ryerson in the movie Groundhog Day.

The scene where Ned, a former classmate, accosts the

star, Bill Murray, has me laughing every time I see it. If you haven't seen it, 'Needle Nose Ned' runs after Bill's character and immediately jumps into a fast-talking sales pitch. I wonder how many people avoid adequate insurance due to the preconceived notion a salesman will sell them a product they don't need.

The reason I initially chose insurance as a career and why I still believe it's important to address as a financial advisor has nothing to do with selling a product. It has everything to do with meeting a family's need for an overall wealth-building and protection strategy. And for this book particularly, preservation of wealth and wealth transfer are very dependent upon insurance solutions as part of the overall financial plan.

## SAFEGUARDING AND STRATEGY

I look at insurance products as a tool that can serve two primary functions: Mitigate financial risks and grow assets for wealth transfer as part of a tax-advantaged plan. My first concern will always be identifying unnecessary threats to assets.

While my career and expertise have expanded and evolved into what it is now, I have experience providing most every major type of insurance for families. As a financial planner, I take my responsibility very seriously to anticipate and protect my clients from many threats to their wealth. Most financial advisors will focus on market fluctuations as a risk to assets. Others will also touch on the importance of planning for inflation and possibly even taxation. I agree these are certainly valid considerations for wealth management planning. However, additional serious risks are overlooked by a majority of financial advisors in the industry.

I consider home, auto, umbrella, medical, long-term care insurance, life insurance, and even fixed index annuities as part of a defensive hedge against risks. Some insurance products also can play more than one role within a financial plan. As an example, there are often opportunities when using life insurance as part of a tax and wealth transfer strategy.

## AUTO & HOME INSURANCE

Starting my career specializing in Property & Casualty insurance gave me a foundation for protection with auto and home coverage. I think it's safe to assume you understand the need and already have policies in place. My only question is, *have you really ever needed to rely on either of these in the event of a major claim?* I'm not referring to a small fender bender or a minor home owner's claim. There are times when home owner's insurance may be needed to cover a major loss of property of $100,000 or more.

Worse, minimum auto-coverage requirements will fall far short of covering the liability in the event of a serious injury or wrongful death claim. In such an event, high net worth individuals can expect to have their personal assets in peril. Can this happen? Well, can you order insurance online without professional guidance? Yes, and yes! And that's exactly why I wouldn't recommend purchasing insurance this way!

Here's my point: We live in an age where we've been taught to treat insurance as a commodity. Advertising campaigns would have you believe that all insurance is the same, and price is the only differentiation. Maybe that's fine for the masses, but I have a warning for you! Insurance is only as good as the coverage stated in the detailed policy and the reliability of the company backing that policy. If you have significant assets to protect, this is not the place to look for the lowest cost insurance. There's more value in having an insurance agent that can assess your personal needs and a company that you can depend upon in a time of need. In my community, there are two major insurance companies headquartered: State Farm and Country Financial. I would recommend either one of them as a solid choice for property and casualty insurance. A good agent will most likely recommend an umbrella policy of $1,000,000 or more to protect against losses above other policy limits. This added insurance may someday be the tool you'll rely on for protecting your wealth.

## MEDICAL INSURANCE

It's undeniable a lack of proper medical coverage caused my family financial hardship when facing the crisis I mentioned. It's shocking how quickly a major medical event can exceed insufficient coverage and proceed to drain hard-earned assets. Coupled with increasing premium costs and ever-greater medical needs as we age, our health care costs are a vital component of our financial picture.

The hope is to have employer health care coverage, or access to a retiree plan, at least until we reach age 65 and become eligible for Medicare. That's a rather simplistic view. We live in a day and age where early retirement is often desired, if not involuntary. Even those lucky enough to rely on their employer plan until Medicare age may be subjected to inflating premiums and co-pays.

Finally, let's address what standard Medicare doesn't cover; dental, vision, hearing, prescription costs, and deductibles. Medicare Supplements and Part D prescription coverage is helpful and available for additional coverage premiums. If you choose a Medicare Advantage plan instead, you might have access to dental, vision and hearing. However, there can be some disadvantages too. Regardless, a comprehensive financial plan must account for these rising healthcare expenses.

# LONG-TERM CARE: THE RISK

One of the most haunting experiences of my career was the May 2017 McLean County Senior Living Expo. The topics covered ranged from the cost of independent senior living facilities to skilled care in nursing homes. I was a featured guest speaker to a packed crowd who were still in shock over the figures for senior living facilities. I still remember how quiet the room was as I laid out the statistics and the likelihood of needing a higher level of care during their lifetime. My job was to now educate them on the high cost of Long Term Care.

Of course, I presented options for long-term care insurance. But the truth is, for many, the opportune time to plan for traditional Long Term Care Insurance had long since passed due to higher premiums as you age. Yes, for many, there were still some options available. But I could see the hopelessness in many of their eyes. Much of what they'd worked for was going to be drained away in their final years.

And it wasn't even entirely their fault! This was one of those key moments affirming my belief the systematic retirement planning system failed to meet the needs of so many! How could it be that the professionals they paid to handle their money never told them to plan for this? Maybe their advisors just followed protocol to make sure they didn't run out of money in retirement. Or, maybe their advisor only dealt with their investments. Maybe they didn't have a plan at all! Do you know what I see all too often from the standard industry advisor? A focus on portfolio growth, or strategies to avoid market losses, while altogether leaving the back door open to a major risk to assets – long-term healthcare expenses!

I understand why people and advisors may wish to cast a blind eye to protecting against this risk. It's costly and gets even more expensive as a person ages. And that's the exact reason why it's so crucial to protect assets! It's the high probability of substantial claims driving the cost. According to Genworth's Cost of Care Survey, every day until 2030, 10,000 Baby Boomers will turn 65 and seven in 10 people will require some form of long-term care services in their lifetime. In Illinois, the cost for a private room averaged about $7,000 per month in 2020, and $6,200 for a semi-private room. The average cost for an assisted living facility in 2020 was $4,575 per month. The statistics for needing some type of long-term care services should be alarming. The point I want to make is that healthcare is a serious financial liability, especially for those interested in passing along assets to heirs. It's critical for a generational wealth plan to account for this.

For those less interested in wealth transfer, with limited assets, they may likely be facing a spend down, leading to Medicaid, which isn't within my field of specialty. When it comes to a LTC strategy, I'm much more concerned for those having assets in the range of $300,000 to $1,000,000. They most likely need to protect those assets for a spouse, or want to protect them for legacy. Those with a net worth of seven figures and above may be able to carry the risk and burden of long-term care expenses without paying for a traditional long-term care policy. However, advanced wealth planning strategies provide better options, which I'll address.

# DETERMINING LONG-TERM CARE COVERAGE

It's important to note that long-term care coverage from Medicare is extremely limited. Medicare Part A will only cover a portion of a skilled nursing facility for the first 100 days. Also, in order to qualify, you must be admitted to the facility within 30 days of a minimum 3-day hospital stay for a related illness or injury. After this, options are 1) Depleting assets until eligible for Medicaid or 2) Long-term care insurance coverage.

A long-term care policy's coverage will usually begin based upon the inability to effectively perform two or three of the six Activities of Daily Living (ADLs). The ADLs consist of bathing, toileting, dressing, eating, continence and mobility.

When a chronic condition exists that prevents one from effectively doing two or more of these basic functions, long-term care coverage may be activated to help with expenses. Insurance carriers will request a doctor's confirmation that an ailment or disability is impairing their ability to be self-sufficient in these tasks, and they will require assistance, either at home or an appropriate facility.

It's not always expected that insurance coverage will begin

immediately. Often policies will have an elimination period before coverage begins. Usually, the elimination period would be 90 days before insurance coverage would begin.

At that point, there are two distinctly different models for covering the expenses: Indemnity and Reimbursement.

A policy that follows the indemnity model is a policy that will pay the maximum benefit regardless of, and without any reference to, actual expenses. So, an approved claim would draw the maximum monthly payout. It's not required for the claimant to pay for that care upfront and submit receipts for reimbursement. Without having to justify the expenses or cost of care, there's the freedom to use the benefits as you see fit for the care you wish and without oversight.

Reimbursement, on the other hand, is exactly what it sounds like. No matter how much the charge is, the policy will only reimburse up to the stated maximum. Costs are incurred, the bills are paid out of pocket and then submitted to the insurance company requesting reimbursement for covered expenses. Usually, the qualifying expenses do not include modification to the home, medical equipment, or most other potential additional expenditures.

# STANDARD LONG-TERM CARE INSURANCE

First, there's no such thing as a 'standard' long-term care insurance (LTCI) policy. Some policies are comprehensive (including most group LTCI policies), building many important features into the base plan–while charging a higher premium. Other lower-priced policies provide only basic coverage but offer you the choice of buying expanded benefits at an additional cost. That's why it's essential when comparing policies to look at both the basic coverage an LTCI policy offers and the optional benefits you can add.

Most LTCI policies today cover a full range of services, including full-time nursing home care (skilled care), part-time nursing home care (intermediate care), or assistance with daily living activities (custodial care). Coverage for mental incapacity (including Alzheimer's disease) is now standard in most policies. Also, a decent basic policy will not require you to spend time in a hospital before receiving long-term care benefits. Moreover, nearly all LTCI policies are renewable, as long as premium payments continue. You should be able to find a basic LTCI package that includes many of these features. If not, find out how much it will cost to add these provisions.

Now that you have an idea of what an acceptable LTCI policy should include, you most likely will want to consider some of the following options and riders, if they aren't included in the basic policy.

- **Home health care** – Most LTCI policies will cover care in alternative care settings, such as the home, adult day-care facilities, and assisted-living facilities. However, this important option is not standard on every policy. Alternative care makes sense when you don't require the constant skilled nursing care that a nursing home provides but still need the services of a health aide at least a few times a week. It can also help you transition from a hospital or nursing home and become self-sufficient.

- **Inflation protection** – When you buy an LTCI policy, you choose a daily benefit level–the amount the policy will pay for your daily care if you need it, but how do you know this will be enough to adequately cover your costs? An inflation rider automatically increases your benefit amount by a specific percentage each year, either by simple interest or compound interest, to help your benefit amount keep pace with rising costs. Five percent is a typical inflation factor. The younger you are when you buy an LTCI policy, the more important inflation protection may be. Keep in mind a simple-interest inflation rider or compound-interest inflation rider can increase your premiums substantially. A possible alternative is to buy a policy with a larger benefit amount today in anticipation of rising nursing home costs in the future.

* **Nonforfeiture of premium feature** – Should you decide you no longer need LTCI or are unable to keep up the premium payments, you may salvage a portion of the policy's benefits or premiums paid. Some contracts contain a return-of-premium option whereby the insurer returns all of the premiums paid beyond a certain date, minus any benefits used up to that point. Others may pay a stipulated percentage of the paid premiums, depending on the number of years the contract was held. Aside from the cash option, another method of preserving the benefits a LTCI policy is through a nonforfeiture conversion. This involves changing the policy to one with a lower coverage amount or coverage for a shorter period of time compared with the original policy. These reduced benefits will be available when needed, and no further premium payments are necessary.

* **Waiver of premium** – This provision allows you to stop paying premiums once you are in a nursing home and the insurance company has started paying benefits to you. Depending on the contract stipulations, the insurance company may waive the premium as soon as it makes the first benefit payment, or the contract may have a waiting period of 60 to 100 days after the onset of nursing

care. Note that the waiver of premium might not apply if receiving home care.

- **Guaranteed insurability** – With this rider, you may increase your level of coverage without submitting to further health questions. This may be important if there's a concern health conditions may change after purchasing the LTCI policy, and you may want to purchase more insurance in the future. This option is particularly attractive if buying a LTCI policy when you're young.

Because any of these add-ons can significantly increase LTCI premiums, there's a need to weigh the importance of these options against the perceived value.

With or without riders, standard long-term care insurance is the most widely known way of paying for long-term care. It's essentially a risk insurance, like auto or home insurance, where you'll pay the premium again and again, hoping you never actually need to utilize it. The higher the risk you are, the more the premiums may cost.

Some insurance professionals will actually advise purchasing a standard long-term care policy at a relatively young age. The upside is a younger person is less likely to be denied coverage due to health conditions. Plus, there's always the possibility, however remote, that an unexpected illness or accident could lead to the need for long-term care. Depending on the policy and the term length, the downside is that what was once an affordable policy may see premium increases that aren't in the budget. For some, that might mean they are faced with terminating their coverage...right when they are likely to need it most. Sadly, there maybe nothing to show for all those years of premium payments.

So, a very real question remains. *How do we still protect ourselves from a likely long-term healthcare event without throwing years of expensive premiums down the drain?*

Fortunately, there are some great alternatives with distinct advantages towards protecting and creating wealth. Many insurance carriers are moving away from traditional, dedicated long-term care insurance to hybrid insurance options that may serve multiple purposes.

# HYBRID INSURANCE FOR LONG-TERM CARE

Life is full of unknowns. Regardless of what the future holds, I intend to educate my clients on how to safeguard their assets from various threats. Obviously, there's a distinct advantage in having one financial vehicle with the versatility to protect from several financial threats. Combine that with the potential for wealth accumulation and tax advantages, and it's no wonder hybrid insurance options are popular.

I consider hybrid insurance policies as a multi-tool, having the capability to be accessed to help pay for long-term care needs. Of course, policies will vary greatly in functionality, but it's possible to select the correct combination of policy and riders to protect against various outcomes. When choosing the proper policy and options, life insurance, and even annuities to a lesser degree, have such a potential.

I want to start by explaining life insurance as a tool to pay for long-term care services. Many times, if I start talking about life insurance to clients, I see their arms go up, waving me off. "I don't need life insurance!" they say. Well, it's not that they necessarily need the *life* insurance protection at that point, but they do need a hedge against a genuine threat to their wealth. The right life insurance policy may help pay for long-term care, home health care, or assisted living. These hybrid policies can achieve this goal utilizing a long-term care rider or an accelerated death benefit rider, also known as a chronic illness rider.

# LTC RIDER VS. ACCELERATED DEATH BENEFIT RIDER

There are two ways to utilize a life insurance policy for LTC: through an actual long-term care rider or an accelerated death benefit rider. As mentioned above, both of these riders are going to pay benefits as a tax-free acceleration of your death benefit. Such withdrawals for LTC will ultimately be deducted from the death benefit. Likewise, coverage is usually limited to the maximum payout of the life insurance policy's death benefit *unless there is an additional benefit for chronic illness.* That's where the similarities end. The differentiators determine which type of claims qualify for a benefit, how the benefits are paid out, and how that rider fee is charged.

An actual long-term care rider is a more comprehensive policy with a more rigorous underwriting process than a standard life insurance policy. Coverage *may* be via indemnity, but in most cases, it will follow the less advantageous reimbursement model. Most accelerated death benefit riders will follow the indemnity compensation model.

There's a distinct advantage that makes these riders worth considering; after the elimination period, a long-term care rider can be used for a temporary inability to perform 2 of the 6 Activities of Daily Living (ADL), while an Accelerated Death Benefit Rider (Chronic Illness Rider) is only triggered upon a doctor certification of most likely permanent or long-term impairment.

Choosing a LTC rider or an ADB rider is dependent upon identifying which rider and policy best align with the viability and goals of the client. I tend to narrow it down based on my clients objective. If gaining the maximum benefit for LTC services is their primary goal, with the death benefit secondary, I will likely look at a policy with a Long-Term Care rider. If maximizing the tax-free death benefit is their primary goal, with the advantage of being able to access that death benefit during their lifetime if needed as secondary, then we are likely to look at a Chronic Illness Rider. It's recommended to work with an insurance advisor experienced with integrating the most suitable policy for achieving a financial plan's objectives.

## ADVANTAGES OF LIFE INSURANCE FOR LONG-TERM CARE

Whole life and term life policies may have a role in protecting families. But when looking for solutions for long-term care, Universal Life insurance (UL) is the best-suited life insurance hybrid because of distinct advantages.

**Permanent policy** – A key feature of such a hybrid policy is having a guaranteed policy for a set premium price with confidence the policy will not be outlived. My recommendation is a policy with coverage until age 102 at a minimum to ensure the family's protection. For those who feel a steady diet of creamed broccoli and mall walking will have them living longer than Betty White, there are policies guaranteed up to age 121!

**Leverage** – As an insurance product, the risk of health care costs are shifted to the carrier. While investments could be used to pay potential LTC costs, it's a dollar-for-dollar scenario. Leveraging insurance offers the advantage of a potentially larger payout than the sum paid in premiums. With a regular premium option, full death benefit is available immediately after an approved policy begins, and access to that death benefit typically has a few stipulations based on the policy, like a 90 days elimination period. Talk about Shifting Risk! After your first premium payment, even if it is one-month premium, you are fully insured!

While a single premium option requires a lump-sum premium payment, no further premiums are due. And, since life insurance is priced by the net amount at risk, you typically save money over the long term. Technically, it is not considered an investment, but the benefit paid upon death or covered healthcare claims is usually much more than the single premium paid.

Policies vary greatly with either option, which allows the financial planner to find a versatile product that best matches the individual's financial needs and budget.

**Flexibility** – No one likes the thought of throwing premiums out the window. Universal life with proper riders has many options for claiming benefits. As such, it's possible to eliminate the 'use-it-or-lose-it risk'. If funds aren't needed for a healthcare-related event, a death benefit is payable to beneficiaries. Additionally, joint policies may offer options that protect both a husband and wife with a single policy. As always, options will vary, based upon the policy.

Tax Advantages – Generally speaking, a life insurance benefit is a non-taxable event. Likewise, so are other benefits derived from a life insurance policy. As such, a universal life policy with an acceleration of a death benefit or health care rider would provide tax-free benefits. This aspect is of extreme importance when calculating the overall benefits of such a policy compared to other wealth-building and asset protection strategies.

*Note: There are situations where policy benefits may not be tax free; this can happen if your policy is a Modified Endowment Contract (MEC). For the purposes of this book, we will not discuss the MEC.*

In summation, life insurance for long-term care may be an excellent solution if you'd like to:

- Potentially increase the value of your estate immediately
- Be able to provide a guaranteed death benefit to your beneficiaries
- Have access to tap into your death benefit If you become chronically ill

# ANNUITIES FOR LONG-TERM CARE

Annuities are great tools for providing a predictable income and avoiding market fluctuations. Some annuities can also be a source of income to provide for long-term care as well. Many policies will allow accelerated access to the cash value for the use of chronic illness expenses. While annuities offer tax-deferred growth, unlike life insurance policies, they don't typically provide protection beyond the account's cash value. When designing financial plans, I would consider annuities better suited for income guarantees in retirement rather than a method for funding long-term care needs.

# ANNUITIES TO MINIMIZE MARKET EXPOSURE

Remember the Dot Com bubble crash? The S&P 500 peaked in March of 2000 at 1,552.87. And over the course of the next 2 ½ years, the market steadily tumbled. Investors that remained in the S&P Market index would have experienced almost a 50% loss by the time it reached a low point of 800.20 in September 2002. But the market did recover. Until…

Remember the housing bubble and the great recession that followed? Yes, finally, in October 2007, the S&P peaked at 1576.09. We know what happened afterward, don't we? The low point of 734.52 in February 2009 meant the S&P 500 once again had given up half its market value. We now know the market came back and matched its October 2007 highs again in March 2013. And it continued a steady upward climb. It's been steady, but has it been reliable?

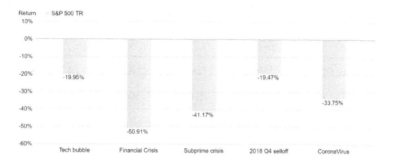

Tech bubble (2000-2001): Deflating of the dot-com bubble caused a prolonged decrease in equity prices.

Financial Crisis (2007-2009): October 2007 - March 2009

Subprime crisis (2008-2009): A rise in subprime mortgage delinquencies led to a financial crisis and recession.

2018 Q4 selloff (2018): Volatility due to raising interest rates, trade disputes and the possibility of recession lead to a global selloff.

CoronaVirus (2020): Virus infection spreads worldwide, threatening to slow down the global economy

Sure, the equities markets show an annualized return of around 10% since inception. *And I strongly believe in market-based investment strategies to meet financial objectives, especially for those with assets approaching seven figures and more.* But I also know there are some who are in a position where market risks could potentially jeopardize their ability to fund their retirement.

Sure, the Dow Jones, S&P 500, and Nasdaq have proven to be very resilient over the long term, despite ups and downs. But what about the short term? What about all the people that retired near the end of 2007, or worse, in March 2000. Facing huge losses the first years into retirement could cause a strain on retirement finances that is difficult to recover from. This is known as sequence of returns risk, and it can have profound implications when seeking a dependable retirement income.

For example, if a 65-year-old had retired in March of 2000, and if he never touched his retirement account invested in the S&P 500 exchange, it would have approximately the same value when he turned 78! Virtually no growth for 12 years! Furthermore, the problem would be exacerbated if it were necessary to periodically access those funds to finance his retirement or to cover his RMDs. The account may never have recovered in his lifetime due to a dual-threat: He would be withdrawing investments that were possibly worth less than when he invested and simultaneously, there would be less money to benefit from the market recovery.

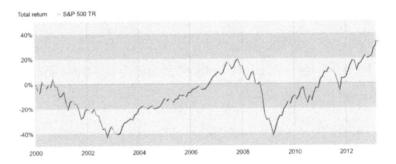

Market drops can be unpredictable. Thus, structuring a predictable retirement plan based 100% upon equities must leave room for variables. We all know stocks go up, and they go down. Thus, we know we cannot guarantee retirement income based solely upon stock predictions.

But, annuities may provide guarantees to remove market exposure risk for cash flow, much like a pension benefit. There are two distinct types of annuities, fixed annuities and variable annuities. In addition, a Fixed Indexed Annuity (FIA) is considered a subclass of the fixed annuity. Variable Annuities (VA) can come with an assortment of fees that are often less than transparent. The account values in a VA fluctuate with the market and income payments may vary based upon the performance of subaccounts. With fixed index annuities, typically, the only fees would be in the form of optional riders. For example, a guaranteed income rider, when chosen carefully, can help meet retirement income goals.

Due to fees and unpredictability, I wouldn't recommend variable annuities in most circumstances. The uncertainty of the valuation of a variable annuity certainly makes it a poor choice for a guaranteed income source. Therefore, I'll be focusing on fixed-index annuities as a source for retirement income.

The beauty of a FIA is it allows to share in some of the upside potential of an equities market without the potential losses in a downward spiraling market. The amount earned is based on the performance of an index such as the S&P or the Dow. The gains are typically locked in each year, and in negative performance years, the insurance company absorbs the losses.

In a year such as 2008, when the S&P 500 suffered a 38.49% loss, a fixed indexed annuity does not lose anything. The value has no gains or losses but just moves sideways. And then, as the market came back up in 2009, there are interest credits again in the annuity. It's a much smoother ride when the market doesn't have to climb back up to where it was before it can venture into the black again.

Here are some of the considerations I consider when I investigate annuities as part of an overall financial plan.

**Purpose** – Often I come across people with several annuities sold to them by various advisors through the years. They often feel frustrated that they have money everywhere without a cohesive plan. This is because they were sold on a product, not a plan for goal achievement. Every financial vehicle should serve a specific function in achieving an overall financial goal. I would not recommend moving forward with an annuity without a thorough analysis and projection of how this change would affect a person's entire financial picture, as well as comparing it to other options.

**Liquidity** – Having access to an adequate portion of investments is vital for navigating emergencies, opportunities, or even to be able to enjoy what you've earned. Annuities are contracts that 'lock-up' the bulk of that investment for years, with stiff penalties for surrendering.

When considering allocating funds to an annuity, realize that future market and interest environments could make the policy look less attractive in the future. However, future market considerations are less relevant if it fits within a plan for income, safety, tax or estate planning. In this case, the vehicle has a specific purpose it was designed to fulfill.

**Growth** – While a fixed index annuity can protect from market drops, it typically will not share in the full upside of the market. The 'spread' or 'cap' can limit growth on the annuity. While some annuities currently may return 5% annually, the average annual S&P 500 growth has been over 10% since inception.

With retirements that could last over 30 years, most retirees will need some growth in their investment portfolio over this span. Having adequate growth in retirement is crucial for most to avoid outliving their retirement. It's important to analyze how an annuity will stand up to inflation, taxation, and increasing healthcare costs. I agree a guarantee that protects money from market fluctuations can be attractive. *But*, only as part of an overall strategy that allows other money to benefit from market gains. I wouldn't recommend investing in annuities without projections to justify it's role in balancing the overall financial picture.

Let's assume that purchasing an annuity makes sense to protect a retiree's income from market fluctuations. How does a retiree know the annuity they're being sold is the best one for their situation? Annuity contracts are extremely complex and can vary greatly. While many have a plethora of attractive features, the pitfalls are often hazed over by insurance salesmen. Here are just some of the options to consider:

**The Insurance Company** – Annuities are not FDIC insured but backed by the strength of the issuing company. Although there is a level of protection with the State Insurance Commission, there are limitations. All insurance companies are rated for financial stability. Warning: an annuity salesman is not required to only sell annuities from highly rated companies!

**Annuity Selection** – Every insurance carrier will have an assortment of annuities available. Variations between annuities include bonuses, how growth is calculated, index options, income options, death benefit options, long-term care allowances, surrender charges, and so much more. Each of these factors combined can make a real impact on financial performance. That's why it's vital to choose an annuity that aligns with financial goals. A financial planner can help select such an annuity and show financial projections that include all income and wealth accumulation.

**Annuity Contract Length** – The commitment can range in length from one year up to ten years or more, with most common being 10 years. Whereas returns on a one-year product aren't strong, committing funds for a lengthy period may mean passing up opportunities or needed liquidity along the way. For example, what happens if inflation sky-rockets and a 10-year annuity's return isn't even keeping pace with inflation? So what's the right length of an annuity? That depends on retirement goals, and if done outside of a financial plan, it's guesswork.

All too often people are making an emotional decision when it comes to purchasing annuities. Some financial advisors may even play upon the fears of a volatile market, leading to a rash decision. I will agree that as people approach retirement and beyond, it may be wise to reduce market exposure and re-allocate investments. And I even agree that often, annuities are a great way to provide retirement income while shielding money from market risk.

However, my strong recommendation is to proceed only as part of an overall allocation plan based upon carefully calculated projections. Only when making a decision based upon all of the facts and data can you be sure it's the right choice. In any case, I wouldn't ever recommend an annuity for 100% of the assets, but simply as a way to protect a portion from losses or create a guaranteed income. And again, this only make sense in certain situations.

# ANNUITIES FOR PROTECTION FROM LONGEVITY

Many people somehow have a preconceived notion that all annuities are awful without fully understanding how the right solution might help financial goals. Depending on their use, that may or may not be accurate. But I find it interesting that nearly everyone who has a pension absolutely loves the sense of security it gives them. In many regards, an annuity can be very similar to a pension. Two key features that enamor people to a pension are that the income is guaranteed to not run out for the rest of their lives, and market drops do not negatively impact the income. This can be emulated with an annuity. Furthermore, it's only one of many options that may be available for receiving income from an annuity.

Aside from certain exceptions, when money is invested in an annuity the investment cannot be accessed without penalty during this accumulation phase. At a date in the future, the annuitant (usually the owner) can choose to annuitize or take income using an income rider (which is different than annuitization). While annuitization can be useful under some circumstances, it isn't the option I typically recommend because you give up access to your money. The option I prefer is utilizing a lifetime guarantee income rider. Just like it sounds, income is guaranteed for the annuitants life, and sometime the life of their spouse too. However, if there is money left in the contract at death, that is typically paid to the beneficiary, such as your children, which likely is not be the case using annuitization.

## LIFE INSURANCE FOR INCOME REPLACEMENT

The loss of a spouse is one of the most devastating events most people will ever face. It's almost a taboo subject no one wants to address. But I don't want to dance around the subject or candy coat it. I've been there with many couples planning for such an event. I've also been there one-on-one with recent widows and widowers. It's emotionally draining for all parties, and after the loss of a spouse, life will never be the same. In the midst of such pain, the last thing a survivor needs to deal with is financial stress. A specialty of mine is helping families prepare for such times in advance as well as assist survivors in picking up the pieces after a loss. It's a critical aspect of financial planning, but for now, I'll just focus on the risk and how important life insurance can be in such circumstances.

It's no secret that losing a spouse can lead to severe income losses and even additional expenses. As a looming crisis, it's essential to create a plan for alleviating potential financial hardship. The strategy required is largely dependant upon the age of the couples. The financial exposure from a spouse's premature death while you are younger with children is entirely different from that of a retired widow with grown children.

**Young Families** – Let's first consider a married couple years from retirement with children still at home. If such a family were to lose a breadwinner, there would be an immediate loss of their earned income. Additionally, the lost years of retirement savings and potential additional child care expenditures must be considered. Something that few people also fail to take into consideration is that tax brackets increase for a single filer, versus a married couple.

Naturally, when someone is younger, you can expect term-life insurance to be relatively inexpensive and have easier underwriting approval. With adequate coverage, your financial plan might provide for the family's needs and even solidify a surviving spouse's retirement funds in the event of an untimely passing. As far as protecting the family in the short term, it will temporarily serve its purpose. However, financial professionals will agree that it does nothing to protect a family over the long-term from rising premiums while failing to build wealth.

Another school of thought is to choose whole life to build wealth while protecting the family. Premiums are higher, but they do not increase with age, and they build wealth. Just make sure the policy doesn't have the potential to lapse if you live too long.

For those seeking multigenerational wealth, here's an opportunity to protect heirs while transferring assets. As I'll explain later, it may be beneficial for a grandparent to purchase a permanent life policy for their child with the grandchild as the beneficiary.

**Mature Couples** – Usually, I'm meeting with this demographic; they are either in retirement or soon to be retired. Here's a common scenario: They arrive at my office for our first meeting, and as they sip their hot coffee, they share with me their fears. Just like so many others, the news has them worried about the direction of the stock market. They're facing retirement, and they don't want to suffer losses to all they've worked so hard to accumulate. They want my advice to protect and guide them.

Of course, their concerns are valid, and I'm happy to help. But how do I look them in the eyes and delicately explain to them an even greater risk they seem to be overlooking? A day may come when one of them is in my office, alone as a widow/widower. And I know the financial consequences of what could happen.

One of the most significant risks for many married couples in retirement is the financial blow when a spouse passes. At first death, there is a reduction to Social Security income for the survivor. Also, for those with a pension, the pension will likely be reduced for the survivor, or it might even cease at first death.

It's a common scenario, but for privacy's sake, I'll use a fictional couple to illustrate the risk: John has a pension, as well as Social Security. Jane raised the children and did not work outside of the household. So she is drawing a spousal benefit, which is half of John's Social Security.

Their total annual income is $81,000. And then suddenly, John passes away. For Jane, the financial picture changes quickly as seen below.

**THIS IS WHAT MAY HAPPEN TO YOUR INCOME WHEN YOUR SPOUSE PASSES AWAY...**

| | | | | |
|---|---|---|---|---|
| John's Pension | $45,000 | | John's Survivor Pension | $33,750 |
| John's Social Security | $24,000 | **John Passes Away** | John's Social Security | $0 |
| Jane's Social Security | $12,000 | | Jane's Social Security | $24,000 |
| Annual Income | $81,000 | | Annual Income | $57,750 |

**Jane's Loss of Income is $23,250, Nearly a 29% Reduction**

First, she may see a change in pension income. Survivor pension benefits vary, but It's not uncommon to have a 25-50% reduction in benefits for the survivor.

And then, there's an additional blow to her income, with a reduction in her Social Security. Jane now receives the equivalent of John's Social Security benefit. Social security awards the higher benefit amount to the survivor, which means Jane's monthly benefit stops.

Her new annual income is now $57,500. A loss of revenue of $23,250 a year! Do you suppose Jane's expenses went down $23,250 a year? Probably not.

I believe one of the most critical obligations I have to my clients is to provide a spousal survival plan. Whether it's needed in one year or in thirty years, both spouses should have confidence the surviving spouse will be provided for.

Having a strategy for a surviving spouse is a crucial element of a financial plan. I recommend a process that explores the advantages of life insurance for a husband and wife's protection when their income and assets may fall short.

My process begins with an analysis of the current coverage. Sometimes, it's often more efficient and cost-effective to replace an existing life insurance policy than add an additional policy to cover a survivor's income gap.

Understanding the basics of how life insurance works is the key to this strategy. Often people will have old life insurance policies. Let's say that John has a life insurance policy that has $100,000 of cash value and $125,000 of death benefit. Upon John's passing, the beneficiary doesn't receive both the cash value and the death benefit! Jane is only entitled to the $125,000 death benefit. This is only $25,000 more than the cash value! Does that seem fair?

Here's how this may happen. Let's assume years ago, John and Jane purchased a whole life policy. When they began paying their monthly or annual premiums, it made sense because from day one, they had an immediate $125,000 death benefit. That's excellent leverage, for a small investment.

But as time goes on, their regular premiums have increased the cash value in the policy and eventually, it grows to $100,000. At this point, how much is the life insurance company actually on the hook for in the event of John's passing?

Only $25,000! That's because $100,000 of that is already John and Jane's! If you've realized the insurance company made more than $25,000 off of your premiums over the years, you're probably right! But the good news is that there may be better ways to leverage the policy's cash value!

There may be a simple way to use their cash value in this scenario and provide a more significant benefit for their family. They may be able to use their existing cash value to fund a new life insurance policy. This is called a 1035 exchange. In this scenario, they would move the $100,000 into a new policy, and it would be counted as a premium. Because mortality tables have changed over the years, life insurance has become less costly to own. This means they will likely be able to increase the death benefit!

So where John had $100,000 in cash value and $125,000 death benefit, he could use a 1035 exchange to transfer those values to pay a one-time premium on a new policy with a much higher death benefit. Please make sure if you use this strategy that there is something to be gained by the new policy!

Scenarios are based upon numerous factors, but there are most likely additional advantages to such a strategy. As I mentioned before, you might be interested in a hybrid policy, meaning you can use it for a death benefit, but you could also use it while living for things such as nursing home care, chronic illness, assisted living, and so on.

So, in addition to a potentially increased death benefit, John and Jane may have a resource to draw upon should they have a need for such care! These options are very attractive when planning because by maneuvering existing assets, we can increase the coverage amount and simultaneously provide coverage for other potential needs. And remember, you aren't limited to using cash value to fund a life insurance policy. You can use other assets too.

Overall, the power of insurance is an incredibly versatile tool to be used to protect property, assets, and income. Proper application can reduce risks to both lifestyle and legacy.

Preservation of wealth must always begin with a solid plan for minimizing threats. Most people are able to comfortably focus on building their wealth for future generations when they feel secure from the aforementioned uncertainties.

And it's no different for the high net worth individuals I'm accustomed to working with. They certainly have the means to overcome many circumstances by merely accessing their assets. However, by strategically leveraging a small amount of their capital, they can protect more of their wealth for the people and causes dear to their hearts.

## References

Resources for annuities:

1. https://mcbeathfinancialgroup.com/do-you-sell-annuities/
2. https://mcbeathfinancialgroup.com/blog/read-this-before-buying-an-annuity/
3. https://mylifesite.net/blog/post/so-ill-probably-need-long-term-care-but-for-how-long/
4. https://www.usatoday.com/story/money/columnist/brooks/2014/09/09/retire-long-term-care-insurance-baby-boomer/14968081/
5. https://www.genworth.com/aging-and-you/finances/cost-of-care.html

# CHAPTER SIX

# Bold Growth

Remember a time before the Coronavirus epidemic when air travelers' only concern for safety was the possibility of a terrorist attack? Rationally, we know that the airlines are doing all they can to prevent the spread of the disease. But during the midst of the pandemic, fliers were crammed into tight spaces with only a mask for protection! If you think this would do anything at all to ease the tension my husband has about flying, you're dead wrong. He had anxiety over flying even before 9/11!

Obviously, some people have no issues with flying. Most people handle it calmly, while others are terrified of the experience. My husband is among the latter.

He doesn't like flying. He sure likes getting to wherever we're going, but he absolutely has no stomach for the ride. Every time there's the slightest bit of turbulence, his face turns ghostly pale, he does a death grip on the armrest and has this look of pure terror on his face. (At least when he flies in the foreseeable future, he'll have a mask to hide behind.) If the other passengers were to judge the outcome of the flight by his mannerisms, it would look like a scene from the movie *Airplane*.

I wish he would just relax and enjoy the ride. But I will give him credit for restraining himself on a memorable flight when something entirely unexpected happened. I'll never forget when a fellow passenger's erratic behavior had me seriously concerned for our safety.

Everyone knows that during take-off, you MUST remain seated. And yet, this was the exact moment a middle-aged man RAN to the front of the plane! Just as the wheels were taking off, he disappeared into the unlit front portion of the cabin, right by the pilot's door, and was intercepted by a very alarmed flight attendant! Let me say, more passengers than just my husband were concerned at this point! Was there a crazy person on board? What was going on? It was dark up front, so we couldn't see, but we knew the flight attendant was talking in a demanding tone. "SIT DOWN!" we all heard…

Just at the point we thought she might be forced to wrestle with him, she somehow calmed him down and got him to sit beside her for the ascent. We heard her assure him a few times that although he **MUST** stay seated now, he could get up in a few minutes.

After we were cleared to move about the cabin, it was apparent what the issue was. *He desperately needed the restroom due to queasiness created from the stress of flying.*

I know unusual things happen on planes, just like they do in markets. We know news headlines can lead to drastic ups and downs on Wall Street, and many investors react to this turbulence. They experience anxiety, fear and often make irrational decisions that adversely affect their investments!

Worse yet, many financial professionals play upon this fear to sell a product to those most vulnerable. A few of the most common fears I see exploited are the fear of outliving their money or fear of market crashes! A knee-jerk reaction is seldom in the best interest of the client for the long run. I will only concede there may be value in a quick financial move if it brings peace of mind. I just believe there is a better way to bring serenity to finances and still include a path for generational wealth building.

# PEACE OF MIND

Every flight begins with pre-flight safety instructions. I'll admit I zone out while my husband is attentively counting the rows to the exit locations. But one part of their demonstration goes against my motherly instincts. The flight attendants clearly state that the masks will drop if we lose cabin pressure, and I'm supposed to secure my own mask before my daughter's!

How could I possibly put myself before my child!?! Logically, we know we must take care of ourselves first, so we have the capability to attend to our children. If a parent passes out before they get both masks on, they are unable to help either themselves or the child.

Generational wealth planning is no different. While mindful of our children, it's important to have stability for our own finances first. Only when we have a solid foundation and free from worries of market conditions and potential threats can we look forward to protecting future generations.

Once we've *Shifted the Risk* as outlined in my previous chapter, most people feel free to pursue an investment strategy focused on building wealth. This process is instrumental in addressing potential threats and laying the foundation to benefit future generations.

Having a foundational plan in place eases most of the common fears prior to creating an investment plan. We have a plan for long-term care and health coverage. We know our living expenses are covered, even in the event of a spouse passing. Once these needs and concerns are managed, most people are more comfortable letting their other assets work for them and pursuing growth.

## INVEST WITHOUT FEAR

Embarking upon a career in financial services as a fresh, naive college graduate, I was certain the courses in finance and insurance would be all I needed. After all, when it comes to finances, everything is purely numbers and logic, correct? Wrong! I should have taken psychology courses! How people feel about their money is even more important than the technical aspects.

Over the course of my career, I've learned how important it is to understand clients' relationships with their financial resources. I listen, ask questions, and often act as a counselor. It's not surprising that husbands and wives often have differences in values and goals with their shared assets. I find myself in a mediation role to clarify shared objectives, quell fears, and come to a mutual understanding.

See, it's my responsibility to create a custom investment plan that meets their objectives within their comfort zone. To help people invest with confidence and have peace with potentially unknown outcomes, it's essential to understand their risk tolerance. As the market is unpredictable, I wouldn't want to create an overly aggressive plan that might have them nervous at times. Some people like a smoother ride, even if it may not get them to their goals as quickly.

It turns out understanding the psychology of investing is a crucial component for better results! There was a time in my education where I thought successful investors were either picking the right individual stocks, timing the market or choosing ETFs or Mutual Funds with the best history. And in practice I've witnessed something entirely different.

There's a key habit I've identified in helping many of the more successful investors succeed. Short and long-term goals are aligned with their attitudes toward conquering objectives. They actually have a feeling of solitude about their investments, throughout fluctuations in values!

Yes, you heard that correctly! Even when their investments have suffered in market downturns, they tend not to panic! But, here's the interesting thing; You don't have to have nerves of steel for this to work. You simply need an understanding of your own behavior and align it to how the market works.

First, we need to examine the relationship of risk and reward between your portfolio and within your own head. Why is this important? Because you have likely projected into the future what you believe your retirement and legacy should look like. Due to the current lifestyle, which is supported by the current income levels it's hard to imagine a different (read: "worse") lifestyle becoming a reality.

If the market takes a downturn, this could immediately induce fear because you're simultaneously equating that to a threat to your legacy and possibly even losing your standard of living!

This often leads to an emotional decision and sabotages long-term investment plans. Unfortunately, changing advisors, jumping out of the market or chasing gains aren't effective solutions. I'm fully aware many advisors offer solutions based upon market predictions. Maybe they have an opinion on how a stock, a sector or even a mutual fund will perform. I must have missed class the day they handed out crystal balls to all these financial advisors. The truth is, any advisor that could predict the future of the market accurately even 60% of the time would be wealthy beyond measure.

There's only one Warren Buffett and even his philosophy is based upon buying value and holding long-term.

Most financial service professionals will talk about diversification, investment strategy, and staying in the market when there's a downturn – because that's what the industry has always focused on. Meanwhile, the family is supposed to hang on and white-knuckle it even while watching news reports of a market plunge! Of course, the ride was fun while the investment advisor was touting double-digit gains, but that doesn't matter when riskier investments eventually do what they do.

And an investor's reaction can be dramatic. There's a psychological principle called the Fear of Losing Everything (FOLE) that causes investors to react and often sell at the worst time. At the root, I believe it's because most advisors and financial media' gurus' are focused on the wrong things, leading the main street investor to focus on the wrong things, too.

There is a better way.

It begins with understanding your personal risk tolerance in relation to the fluctuations in the market. Then you need to align your investment portfolio to match that risk tolerance. That way, even if the overall market loses significant value, you will stay in the market without locking in long-term losses. This is because your portfolio is balanced to match your personal, individual risk tolerance.

Now, that's easily stated, but how do we impartially identify how someone will react? How do we measure that objectively? As I mentioned before, during conversations with clients, understanding their goals and feelings about money is critical in successfully managing their investment portfolio. But still, that could lead to a guess in actually attributing a mathematically quantified 'number' to their disposition.

And guessing doesn't work for me and guesswork shouldn't be something investors rely upon when it comes to planning their financial future. Fortunately, advances in financial technology have bridged the gap between psychology and quantitative analysis! The breakthroughs have delivered advanced algorithms designed to assist in assigning investors a risk score. Yes, an actual personal risk score that ranges from 1-100!

At my firm, McBeath Financial Group, we utilize our *Technology Empowered Advisor Method* (TEAM) approach. One of the specific advanced software tools we utilize is data-driven in matching and minimizing investment risk.

We can even look at existing assets and determine what the risk number is of those assets. That number is determined based on examining potential swings from growth and losses, volatility, looking at fees, looking at dividend income, historical models, and several other data points.

The beauty is, we are analyzing the risk and setting a corresponding score to current and recommended investments. This process allows an investor to match their portfolio with one that reflects their personal mindset.

Then, when we work towards matching the investments, sometimes we'll adjust the portfolio's volatility towards reducing risks. Other times, if a person has a higher risk tolerance, we'll work towards raising the upside potential. We'd all love to have high returns with no risk, but outside of fantasy, it's a matter of optimizing return for a given amount of risk.

As a reader of my book, feel free to take your own free Risk Assessment Analysis. You can access the online questionnaire here: http://mcbeathfinancialgroup.com/portfolio-risk-score

Through this free online assessment, you'll find the ideal risk level for your own portfolio. With a little extra help, you can also identify the level of risk you currently have in your portfolio (Hint: It might be higher than you think or want.)

The whole point is, when your portfolio adheres to a fluctuation range within your comfort zone, you're more likely to allow the markets to work for you with less stress. This generally means there's less likelihood of making bad investment decisions under duress.

## STICK TO THE PLAN?

When the investment strategy mirrors an individual's comfort zone, it seems it would be fairly logical to stay the course with a well-conceived plan. But let's be serious. We're human! We can make mistakes. Sometimes we out-think ourselves, or maybe we experience a change in circumstances. Other times our priorities or values change.

There's another common factor at work that often has us second-guessing an established investment strategy. While the plan might have felt like a fit when created, a cognitive bias can later alter our position. A psychological phenomenon called recency bias causes us to give more weight in our judgment to more recent events. Our preferences can easily be swayed based upon the most current market trends!

In light of all this, does it make sense that plans should change? Yes and no. It depends on why there is a change. As mentioned before, a good investment advisor will meet with clients regularly to gauge if there's a shift in their risk tolerance. It happens, and an adjustment may be warranted.

However, if an emotional reaction causes a drastic abandonment of a long-range strategy, it may prove costly in the long run.

Loss aversion is a cognitive bias, where we are more afraid of losing than we are attracted to gaining. When the market begins to drop, and news is grim, it's human behavior to consider abandoning a long-term investment strategy and selling some of your portfolio. However, the worst time to sell is while the market is down. With worries of further losses, we justify our decision by 'adjusting our strategy'. Alternately, when the market hits record peaks, it tends to make people nervous, as they know eventually it must come down. Either way, it certainly sounds logical to sell when the valuations are peaking and buy back in at the market bottom, right? The reality is that trying to time the market may be the most effective way to sabotage your investment goals.

The reason this strategy fails is very straightforward; In order to time the market, you have to both sell at the right time and buy back in at the right time. Also, since markets don't move in a straight line, you have to know which direction the market is actually trending. Even the best experts are routinely wrong in predicting the direction. Finally, it's important to not miss the days where the market sees its largest gains. Analysis of previous markets can show the dramatic impact of missing only a few of the year's best trading days.

Let me explain some of the potential outcomes of trying to time the market. One potential development after selling would be the market goes up. You could miss some of those largest gain days. This is also dangerous because at what point do you enter back into the market? Obviously, you want to wait until it's lower than where you sold, but who knows when that will be? And even at that point, how do you know how deep the valley is?

But what if you got lucky? Let's say the day after you sold your investments, the market trended downward. The next question is again, how do you know when it's hit bottom? You don't. There may be several large gaining days missed as it regains its losses. Furthermore, as the market fluctuates, what if the market gains actually surpass the point where you originally sold, instead of continuing downward. At what point do you concede and jump back into the market at a higher point? All I can say is, better have an ample supply of anti-acid and maybe some anti-anxiety meds for that ride!

A comprehensive financial plan should be designed for peace-of-mind, regardless of what the market does. Following the steps outlined in previous chapters tends to minimize any anxiety-causing risks. There's usually a feeling of freedom and confidence in embracing a long-term strategy for investments with such a foundation in place.

With that said, does it make sense to adjust the strategy within a comfort level? Yes, there are certainly adjustments that can be made to minimize risks if feeling uneasy. Seldom does that necessitate bailing out of the market altogether, but perhaps adjustments to reduce risk. When the broad indexes sometimes encounter greater losses, a well diversified portfolio will likely experience a lesser impact.

But how do you know if you're experiencing a short-term reflex to recent events rather than needing to adjust your portfolio – *and investment plan?* This is one of many circumstances when there is value in having a trusted advisor who can help sort out feelings and identify valid concerns.

# BENEFITS OF AN ADVISOR RELATIONSHIP

I believe an ongoing relationship with a trusted financial advisor to be one of the most important keys to successful and stress-free investing. It's a common misconception that fee-based financial advisors are paid their fees merely to pick the right stocks, bonds, mutual funds, ETFs, or other investments. While helping match an investment portfolio is undoubtedly important, it's just one of the many advantages of having a professional money manager working for you.

Benefits that can be measured both quantitively and emotionally are why investors depend upon the guidance and relationship with their financial advisor. They derive multiple benefits they feel justify and outweigh the advisory fees.

**Diversification through strategic asset allocation and adjustments** – Starting with the most obvious duty of a financial advisor is finding the right mix of investments to maximize return for a given amount of risk, based on risk tolerance and goals. In addition, there is ongoing investment management, oversight and monitoring that keeps the plan on the right track. Just as objectives and circumstances may change, markets and financial products are fluid as well. A professional portfolio manager can help guide you through both bear markets and bull markets. Often advisors have a strategic partnership with a dedicated investment committee that consistently reviews portfolios from a list of thousands of investment funds. Then, extensive screening and analysis will determine the makeup of a customized portfolio.

**Access to a professional financial advisor for guidance** – Maybe even more important than adjustments to a portfolio is having the guidance from an advisor to direct when NOT to make changes. Many investors see a growth year like 2019 and are tempted to chase those gains, taking on additional risk. Without an advisor to explain how that might impact their portfolio in the event of a drastic market drop, they may risk their entire retirement. Likewise, having an advisor as a sounding board can help alleviate fears during the market bumps along the way. These conversations happen as a result of an advisory relationship.

**Fluid financial planning for life changes** – It's paramount to have a relationship with an advisor that prioritizes you as a current client versus constantly pursuing new business. I'm always in awe of the advisors who continually host dinner seminars and wonder how they can possibly serve an endless influx of clientele adequately! An advisory relationship should ensure current clients have top priority.

When existing advisory clients need guidance, require updates to their financial plan or have questions, they should have first consideration for the advisor's time and resources. The regularly scheduled meetings often reveal new life circumstances that necessitate vital changes to a financial plan and/or investment plan.

Such circumstances may require calculating an employer's downsizing offer, considering a relocation, or maybe even dealing with a health or family issue. In some cases, the life event may be the loss of a loved one. Many of these events can change the trajectory of your retirement course. During these life events, it's vital to have an advisor that will patiently listen and guide. From there, changes may be needed that require new analysis, recommendations, and a reconstructed investment/financial plan.

**Relationship with ongoing support for family** – I believe the most significant value of a trusted advisory relationship is revealed when there is a loss of a spouse. I know so many who have felt comforted knowing that their spouse will have someone to lean on for financial affairs in their time of need.

We all know that statistically speaking, it is common for a wife to outlive her husband, and it also isn't uncommon, especially in the boomer generation and older, for the husband to handle many of the financial affairs. But what happens when he's gone? At such a time, there's solace in having a pre-existing relationship with the person familiar with advising on financial affairs through the years. There's peace knowing the trusted advisor is in a position to step in and immediately assist with all those financial matters during a time when you, or your survivor, don't want to have to think about it.

Most people don't want to think about such an event; thus they can't fathom what a surviving spouse might have to endure. It can take months helping widows/widowers sort out financial affairs if there wasn't a plan or an advisor in place when their spouse passed away. Often, to get accounts properly transferred to the spouse, it's necessary to navigate complex and tedious procedures and paperwork involving financial institutions, the IRS and/or the state. Beyond that, there is often expertise that is required to avoid costly mistakes and tax implications. Quite simply, it's a much easier process when everything is accounted for and on record with a third party, who, as your advisor, can tend to those tasks and help in every way to ease the burden while offering ongoing guidance.

**Peace of mind** – Finally, I think what my clients value most is the relationship. They know they have a trusted advisor to lean on at all times, now and the future, for them and their family. Life has a way of throwing us the unexpected. We see issues with employment status, family issues, health, and of course, tax and legislation changes no one could predict. During these times, having an advisor in your corner who understands your whole financial picture can help guide your financial decisions, navigate paperwork, or be a counselor. Monetarily, making the right decisions can have a considerable impact on your estate, but it's the reassurance and peace of mind that are also important. When needed, people would prefer to meet with an advisor that's familiar with them and their financial situation instead of no advice or advice from a stranger.

# CONFIDENCE TO SOAR

Just like flying, there's always the remote possibility of the unknown and unexpected when it comes to investment accounts. Some people may see staying grounded as an option. Cash, Certificates of Deposit (CDs), money markets, and annuities are often seen as a way to avoid market risks.

But are they without risks?

While protected from the market, such safe money options are still subject to inflationary depletion of value and other risks. So, while avoiding market-based investments may seem like a safe strategy, it's actually playing a game hoping not to lose. But is it really protecting from losses? Couldn't opportunity costs be considered losses? It could be argued that the actual losses are the difference between the returns of the safe investments versus the market-based investments.

Comparatively speaking, the S&P 500 historically has experienced approximately a 10% annual return since its inception in 1926. That's a solid track record. You can do your own checking to compare it to a current CD rate or annuity rate, but it can be shown to grow assets at a far greater rate in the long run. For generational wealth building, I feel very comfortable recommending a long-term moderate to growth strategy simply because we aren't concerned about short-term fluctuations. When short-term needs are covered, we are free to focus on the growth for generations to come.

When we fly, most of us are confident of the outcome, regardless if there's a little turbulence along the way.

Similarly, when choosing an investment plan, we've carefully calculated the risks and rewards so we can relax, knowing the destination is in sight. And like a great flight attendant, having an advisor along to guide the journey can make the trip more relaxed and enjoyable.

## References

1. https://www.kiplinger.com/article/investing/t031-c032-s014-psychology-of-stock-market-and-investment-decision.html

2. https://www.investopedia.com/ask/answers/042415/what-average-annual-return-sp-500.asp

# CHAPTER SEVEN

# Celebrate Abundance

*"Remember that the only purpose of money is to get you what you want, so think hard about what you value and put it above money."* – **Ray Dalio**

There's no shortage of quotes about money from rich and famous people. I almost reconsidered sharing this quote from Ray Dalio until I learned more of his history. He's renowned as the multi-billionaire founder of a hedge fund company, Bridgewater Associates. So, he may be one of the 100 wealthiest men on the planet, but in my opinion, that alone isn't enough to garner my respect. Often, the uber-wealthy have a disconnect when it comes to the values surrounding money.

What does impress me is his journey. Many people don't realize he was self-made and struggled early in his career. At one point, he had to ask his father for a $4,000 loan just to pay his family's bills! He readily admits to poor career judgment. But he bounced back in a big way and never forgot who he was. Sure, along the way, there were mansions, private jets, and all the luxuries unfathomable wealth can provide. But what strikes me is how he has given billions to charity and written books to pave the way for other's success. It seems he truly does understand the value and purpose behind money.

## WHAT'S YOUR PURPOSE?

All our lives, we've been told how important it is to accumulate wealth in our working years. Ostensibly we've been directed to set money aside for retirement. Is it surprising that it's so hard for the young to follow the common wisdom of saving, especially if they struggle to make ends meet? Even for high earners, it's a hard sell to give up instant gratification. A shiny new vehicle, fancy vacations, or other luxuries have a stronger appeal than the promise of having money decades down the road. They often feel they will be 'too old' to enjoy their savings, even if they live that long! Maybe the messaging is wrong? Again, perhaps a purpose beyond providing retirement income needs to be delivered earlier in life.

For those of us that have had the discipline, wisdom and/or fortune to accumulate financial resources, we often find ourselves at the end of the journey without a direction. Beyond retirement, how would you like your wealth to serve you? Ask yourself, "What do I want?" This might feel odd when for so long the focus has been on what you **don't** want; nobody wants to stress about financial security or run out of money in retirement.

So maybe it's time to stop and just think, what do you want out of life? An abundant lifestyle, vacations, a particular automobile, or boat, or maybe even a vacation home? Others want to promote a cause dear to their hearts. A common goal is as simple as having the resources to enjoy time with family. I also think it's safe to assume that if you're reading this book, you're very interested in passing along your wealth to the ones you love and/or charities you support.

What if you could enjoy your desires now, under your terms? When I think of success, it's the joy I see in some of my clients who are enjoying their lives to the fullest now. We've worked together to help them control their finances, not be controlled by their money. Through planning, they've achieved the freedom of enjoying a lifestyle they are comfortable with and more. In addition, they have the satisfaction of seeing their legacy plan in action! Most people don't realize that this isn't a pipe dream that only the wealthy can attain, but it does require discipline in following a plan.

# ENJOY YOUR WEALTH RESPONSIBLY

Before I move on, I do want to offer some words of caution. While I wish for people to have a sense of freedom when it comes to money, that does not mean financial irresponsibility. Often, after a lifetime of saving, suddenly unlocked retirement accounts may feel like the magical pot of gold at the end of the rainbow. I cannot emphasize enough the balancing act that needs to happen with the use of these resources. Squandered savings aren't easily replenished when no longer earning income from employment!

The transition to retirement life in itself is an adjustment. Many people at this stage have access to more money than they've ever had before in their lives. At the same time, without a work calendar, they have more free time to enjoy the money. While assumptions may calculate a decrease in spending during retirement, it doesn't always happen this way! Many retirees see an increase in expenses from healthcare costs, as well as food and entertainment!

Unrestrained free spending is particularly hazardous early in retirement. Most financial plans will be based upon the growth of investments during retirement. Tapping an excessive amount of these retirement accounts earlier could mean that your money will not last your lifetime. This is of particular concern if you are drawing down at an excessive rate during a market downturn. The distributions taken from an account while the market is down won't be available to experience the market recovery, which will lead to a much quicker draw-down rate! And finally, loose spending early may create spending habits where it's more challenging to adjust to a tightened budget later.

More often, though, when people reach retirement age, I see another scenario that's equally as heartbreaking. It's the people who have the means to achieve their dreams but just don't see that they can. It's the sad case of those working past the time they wish to retire out of fear. Others have retired but are afraid to enjoy what they've saved so long for. They absolutely have the means, but nobody has shown them how to live out their dreams with confidence!

There's no reason why so many people should live in fear and give up the life they should be enjoying.

As I've said, financial control means you control your money, so it doesn't control you! It's a balancing act that begins with assessing what's truly important and plotting a financial map to achieve it.

## PLAN TO SPLURGE

At first glance, it may seem that budgeting and financial planning take the fun and spontaneity out of life! Nothing is further from the truth! Planning and budgeting should allow you to enjoy your priorities *without guilt*.

"Treat yo' self!" is one of my favorite lines from the television series *Parks and Recreation*. Characters in the series repeatedly use this line to justify a day of unbridled pampering and spending. Sure, it was reckless to watch, but at the same time, it was therapeutic for the characters experiencing it. Despite the comedic element, there is some sound wisdom behind the phrase. You've probably earned the right to "Treat yo' self" occasionally, and it should be part of the plan.

A great income plan in retirement shouldn't only include a paycheck for responsibilities! Plan for a 'play' check, which is money outside the budget to enjoy as you wish, whether it's clothes shopping, golfing, restaurants, spoiling grandkids, or little getaways.

## FUNDS ON DEMAND

While these little splurges are regularly available through a spending plan, sometimes life requires a little more capital. Whether it's an unplanned expense or a bigger purchase that fulfills your heart's desire, it's important to have access to a certain portion of your assets when necessary.

One of the concerns many people have about their investments is having access to their money if needed. Let's face it; people don't want to be told they can't easily get to their own money when they want it! I fully agree that everyone should have sufficient liquid money available for whatever life might throw their way, but liquidity requires trade-offs. There's a delicate balancing act between three distinct monetary categories: safety, liquidity, and growth. We illustrate this using a triangle with Growth at the apex, and Safety and Liquidity at the base. It's important that we define Safety as the preservation of principal, so no market exposure. We all wish for the perfect single financial product that will offer the advantages of all three categories. But in the real world, we can choose the advantages of the two most important categories while accepting some limitations on the third. Fortunately, with the right strategy, we can create balance within a financial plan and overlap all three categories.

The most liquid funds would be money kept in a checking or savings account. I'm not against a healthy balance for monthly living expenses, plus any other minor needs that may pop up. Just remember, these accounts earn next to nothing. Choosing to have an excessive amount here equates to choosing the Safety and Liquidity categories, which means you will sacrifice the Growth strategy by having an excessive amount here. There's also a risk of losing purchasing power by not keeping up with inflation.

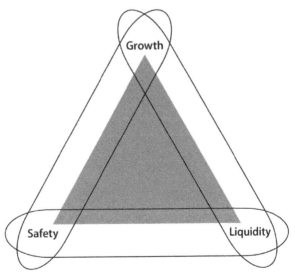

Many choose money markets as a 'safe' option for money that's relatively liquid. Again, the earnings can be dismal, so understand what's sacrificed for 'safety and liquidity'.

CD's, Fixed Annuities, and Fixed Indexed Annuities offer protection of principal, as well as more growth opportunity than bank accounts, however, they are often poor choices for liquidity. There are usually penalties for early withdrawals, although most annuities allow for access to some funds without penalty. Therefore, it is important to first have sufficient funds set aside for potentially larger capital needs when working with these options. Again, these are considered 'safer' investments with growth opportunity, but your liquidity is limited. But if you know that your liquidity needs are met, you can trade-off some unneeded liquidity for growth.

Mutual Funds, Exchange-traded funds (ETFs), stocks, and bonds primarily focus on growth. You might be wondering why I don't consider bonds as part of the Safety category. My reason for this is that if it's necessary to sell the bond while the market is down, there's a loss; a bond must be held until maturity to avoid a loss of principal. Therefore, bonds don't belong in the Safety category, although they can be low risk. Generally speaking, all of these investment vehicles fall into the Growth/ Liquidity category; because there is a risk of loss, the safety category is sacrificed. I consider most of these investments to be fairly liquid in that funds can usually be converted to cash and arrive in a bank account within a few days. Of course, doing so during a market downturn may lock in losses.

When looking at liquidity, I prefer the advantages of ETFs over mutual funds. Mutual Funds often experience trading fees and front load or back-end load fees. This means investments in mutual funds may have fees when initially investing and/or accessing funds, so jumping in and out of these investments quickly would impact overall returns or possibly mean losses. ETF's do not have load fees or redemption fees, among other advantages. Easy access to funds without penalty means ETF investors don't feel 'locked-in' to an investment.

Although there are other investments and financial products I have not specifically named, if you look closely at them, you will find they will typically fall into two out of the three categories.

# GIVING WHILE LIVING MAKES SENSE!

Of course, we'd all love to experience the appreciation of our benefactors after we're gone, right? Who wouldn't want to be a fly on the wall as your estate attorney reads the will to your family? How great would it be to see how your actions benefit future generations and causes? Mostly though, we resign ourselves to knowing our dearest wishes will endure beyond our lives.

It's a safe assumption you are reading this book because you are generous in spirit and care about others. While many are motivated by self-preservation or because they've been indoctrinated to only pursue nothing more, most people will not look beyond their own retirement needs. But for those who are looking at the bigger picture, Legacy Planning is a selfless pursuit that looks beyond the personal needs of retirement planning. It's the joy of sharing what you've earned to benefit others in a meaningful way.

Would you be interested to know you don't have to wait? Instead of thinking about legacy in terms of after your gone, think about "Giving While Living". Certain estate planning strategies can allow you to experience the joy of giving while you are still living!

*Some of the greatest joy is found in adjusting a "legacy" plan to a "Giving While Living" plan so one can see their loved ones, or charities, enjoying their gifts while they are still living.*

Giving to your loved ones or charities while you are living, as well as legacy planning, is a reward for taking the time to complete a financial plan. These are both "giving" plans. It should be celebrated.

It's great to take those family vacations, spoil your grandkids at Christmas, and regularly contribute to your church or charity. By having a comprehensive financial plan, you can delve more deeply into strategic wealth transfer in a way that may benefit you, as well as your benefactors.

"Giving while living" strategies can vary dependent upon the individual's unique goals and financial circumstances. Some will want to include charitable contributions as part of their legacy, and I'll address those strategies in chapter 11. For now, I'll share a few strategies for transferring wealth to family while still living. These are excellent ways to enjoy your "giving" plan in action.

**Gifting** – Gifting is perhaps the most straightforward way to share with those you care about while still living. As of 2021, the current maximum annual amount each individual can give is $15,000 without having to file a Gift Tax Return.

Anything surpassing this will apply to the IRS lifetime exemption, which is currently $11.7 million, and will require a gift tax return to be filed. It is important to note that a married couple may split their gifts, doubling their allowed annual gift tax exclusion amount. This means that together they can give $30,000 to any one individual for the calendar year. This limit will need to be reviewed annually.

**College Education** – Providing for children or grandchildren's education is an excellent option for giving while living. In addition to cash gifts, tuition can be paid directly to a college with no limits. Please note that both gifting and tuition payments may adversely affect the ability to qualify for student loans.

529 College Savings Plans are another prevalent path to provide for future generation's educations. A 529 plan offers federal and state tax benefits and high limits. Savings accumulate tax-deferred and distributions are tax-free when used for qualified college expenses. Although these investments count towards the $15,000 limitations for gifting as outlined above, lump-sum options can make this strategy attractive.

**Children's Life Insurance** – Undoubtedly, life insurance can provide for loved ones after passing, but few people capitalize on the advantages of purchasing a policy on grown children. Purchasing Universal Life insurance for your children is an excellent wealth transfer strategy that protects their younger family. It offers immediate tax-free death benefits if they pass away, and *potentially can provide tax-free retirement income* for them later in life! This is an advanced and highly effective strategy for reducing excessive tax liabilities over multiple generations.

There are many options available, but the right strategy can significantly increase the impact of the gifts. When you as a benefactor can potentially reduce a future tax burden, more assets can remain in investments that may grow, potentially leaving a larger inheritance to pass along.

Depending on how the estate plan is structured, a larger inheritance may push the boundaries of state and federal estate tax exemptions. At the federal level, in 2021, the tax assessment begins at 18% for an estate above $11.7 million, quickly scaling to 40% on all assets above $12.7 million. Additionally, you can expect a state Estate Tax depending on your state of residence. There is a graduated estate tax for Illinois, starting when an estate reaches $4 million, with a top rate of 16% at $10.04 million. Many don't understand that once your estate reaches $4 million, nearly the entire estate is taxed at graduated levels, not just the amount over $4 million.

There are currently proposed tax increases in motion to drastically lower the federal estate tax exemption thresholds and increase the tax rates. The intention is to capture more revenue during the wealth transfer stage. It remains to be seen how new tax laws will ultimately materialize, but it's clear the government has plans for your money if you don't. The question is, who is going to enjoy spending your hard-earned money? Wouldn't you like to choose? Maybe you'd rather enhance your lifestyle, pass more on to heirs, or donate to charity rather than pass more of your estate on to the IRS.

Most of us want to provide the best we can for our families. Overall, a well-conceived giving strategy allows more control in how your money passes on and how you want to utilize it while you are living to enjoy that time with your family. Often, giving while living will help you maximize wealth transfer due to potential estate tax savings in the future.

### References

1. https://www.wsj.com/articles/estate-and-gift-taxes-2020-2021-heres-what-you-need-to-know-11617908256
2. https://www.kiplinger.com/taxes/601639/estate-tax-exemption
3. https://smartasset.com/estate-planning/illinois-estate-tax
4. https://www.investopedia.com/terms/s/stretch-ira.asp
5. https://www.nytimes.com/2021/03/12/business/estate-tax.html

# CHAPTER EIGHT

# CHARTED LEGACY
## by Chad A. Ritchie, Esq.

N ow that you have accumulated your estate assets, the next question is often how should those assets be legally passed to the next generation? Your estate plan is the map you leave behind that says who inherits your assets at the time of your death. It is a map that determines the kind of legacy you will leave to your family and loved ones.

Without this estate plan "map," you could be leaving your family and loved ones a complicated mess to deal with as they try to administer your estate. Your estate may have to pay unnecessary taxes or go through a long Probate court process that could have been avoided. Worst of all, your assets may not be distributed to who you ultimately want them to go to.

As an estate planning attorney in Illinois, I've reviewed, analyzed, and drafted hundreds of estate plans over the years. Yet, as many people as I've served, I know countless more aren't receiving the legal guidance that would benefit them and their families. Why is that when the stakes are so high?

People often simply procrastinate on having their estate plan created or updated. Maybe they have good intentions to protect their families, but the process might be intimidating and overwhelming. Perhaps they don't realize the importance. Many other people just don't know where to start with the process.

It's my goal to demystify the process and provide some clarity with a basic, plain English overview of how estate planning works by walking you through the same educational process and analysis I utilize with my new estate planning clients.

A good estate planner will begin by analyzing the client's assets from an estate planning point of view. In my practice, I have a process that helps me educate my clients on whether they need a "Will-Based" estate plan or a "Trust-Based" estate plan.

When learning about how estate planning works and what kind of estate plan is needed, it's advised to take small steps and focus on one estate planning concept at a time. The first estate planning concept we need to discuss is the difference between a will-based and a trust-based estate plan. Ultimately one plan must be chosen over the other. Once you understand how this decision is made, estate planning becomes so much simpler, and everything falls into place.

# WILL-BASED PLANS VS. TRUST-BASED PLANS

Many people think that estate planning is just having a Last Will and Testament prepared and signed. The first thing most people tell me when they first meet is that all they need is a "Simple Will." As you will see in this chapter, determining the type of estate plan someone needs (even if it is a "simple will") first requires clearing up some widespread Estate Planning misconceptions about Wills.

**Wills** – A "Will" is a document that you sign that says who inherits your "Probate Assets." Probate Assets are assets you own just in your name, and they **DO NOT** have beneficiary designations. I'll provide more detail later.

**A Will-Based Plan** – is where your Will is the main estate planning document, and you don't have a Trust as part of your estate plan. A Will-Based Plan is generally for less complex estates. If you have complex assets, a complex family situation, minor children, or want to control how your assets are used after your death, then you will need to have a Trust-Based Plan rather than a Will-Based Plan.

There are two main misconceptions about Wills that most people have:

## Will Misconception No. 1:

The first misconception is that most people think that a Will controls who inherits **ALL of the assets they own at the time of their death.** This is not true. A Will **DOES NOT** control assets that have beneficiary designations or assets that are owned jointly with right of survivorship.

*Key Concept – Wills: Beneficiary designations trump whatever a Will states. Jointly owned assets trump whatever a Will states.*

For example, someone's Will could say all assets will go to a spouse upon passing. BUT suppose there is a retirement account that names a beneficiary other than the spouse. In that case, that other named beneficiary will receive the retirement account assets despite the Will saying all assets should be distributed to the surviving spouse. So, to re-iterate – beneficiary designations and joint ownership trump whatever someone's Will says.

## Will Misconception No. 2:

The second big misconception people have about Wills is that they think their estate will avoid Probate just by the fact that they have a signed Will. This is not true. All a Will does is say who inherits your **Probate Assets**. A will does not control whether your estate will have to go through Probate or not.

We will discuss how your estate can avoid Probate in more detail later.

**Key Concept – Wills:** *Having a signed Will <u>DOES NOT</u> automatically make your estate avoid Probate upon your passing.*

**Trusts** – A Trust is an agreement that someone signs in which assets are held in the name of the Trust for the benefit of one or more persons.

The peopled named in the Trust to benefit from the Trust

assets are called "Beneficiaries". Trust beneficiaries should not be confused with beneficiary designations. Remember, assets that have a named beneficiary will trump both a Will and a Trust. You can, however, name your Trust as a beneficiary of certain accounts.

Every Trust also names a "Trustee" – the person who has the authority to manage the trust assets and distribute trust assets to the Beneficiaries. The Trustee must follow the terms of the Trust when distributing assets to the beneficiaries.

The person that signs the trust document and creates the Trust is called the "Grantor".

When Grantors create a Trust, they can decide if they want to give themselves the authority to amend or revoke (terminate) the Trust later if they want to. This type of Trust is called a "Revocable Living Trust". Most people that create trusts for themselves have Revocable Living Trusts.

The other main type of Trust is called an Irrevocable Trust. These are trusts that do not allow a Grantor to amend or revoke the Trust in the future; the terms of the Trust are set in stone.

**Key Concept – Trusts:** *Revocable Living Trusts have the flexibility to be amended, and assets in the Trusts can be* *controlled long after the original Grantor passes away. Revocable Living Trusts are much more flexible in their terms than Wills. Irrevocable Trusts do not allow anyone (including the Grantors) to amend or revoke the Trust in the future – the terms are set in stone. Irrevocable Trusts are desired for more complex estate planning purposes – such as asset protection or estate tax reasons.*

## PROPER ESTATE PLANNING

It's important to ensure an estate plan is the right estate plan based upon the client's family, assets, and estate planning goals.

Sometimes a simpler Will–Based estate plan is all someone needs. Other times a more complex Trust-Based estate plan is needed. I have new clients come to see me with the idea that they need a Trust because of something they read on the internet or because their brother-in-law has a Trust and therefore, they need one too. After the analysis process, sometimes it turns out they only need a Will-Based estate plan.

Other times a new client comes in thinking they only need a "Simple Will," and as we analyze their estate, we find they need a Trust.

Either a Will-Based or Trust-Based estate plan can be proper – as long as it is the right estate plan for you, your family, and your estate planning goals.

So, how do you decide if a Will-Based estate Plan or a Trust-Based estate plan is needed? To be objective and provide clarity, I utilize our Estate Plan Continuum™ chart.

# THE ESTATE PLANNING CONTINUUM™

Below is a diagram that I call the Estate Plan Continuum™. This diagram shows the various types of estate plans– starting with the most simple ones on the left and gradually increasing in complexity until you get to the far right with the most complex ones.

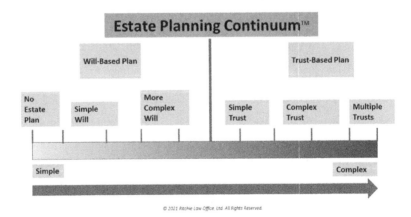

Estate plans can be very simple, or they can be very complex – depending on three things. The assets involved, the family, and individual estate planning goals.

**No Estate Plan** – On the left-hand side of the Estate Planning Continuum™ is the simplest estate plan possible – which is no formal written estate plan at all. Every state has its own laws that say who would inherit an estate without a signed Will or Trust.

In Illinois, if someone dies without a Will, the order of who inherits your Probate Assets are as follows:

*1* If you have a surviving spouse but no children, then everything to your surviving spouse;

*2* If you have surviving children but no spouse, then everything to your children;

*3* If you have a surviving spouse AND surviving children – then ½ of your Probate Assets to your surviving spouse and one-half of your Probate Assets divided equally among your children;

*4* If you have no surviving spouse and no surviving children – then to your parents and siblings in equal shares, but if only one parent survives, that parent receives a double share.

Many people do not want the third rule set forth above to be their estate plan. I have seen tough cases where one-half of a deceased parent's estate went directly to young children (no children's Trust) instead of all going to their surviving spouse. The deceased parent didn't have a Will; therefore, they had to follow the State of Illinois' estate plan.

Other states' laws will differ from the rules above in one way or another – but the point is if you don't have your own estate plan – your state has an automatic estate plan for you and your assets – that you probably won't like.

**Will-Based Estate Plan** – The next simplest plan is the Will-Based estate plan. Notice the various types of Will-Based Estate Plans available as we move across the Estate Planning Continuum.

Will-based Estate Plans are limited because all a Will does is transfer Probate Assets to the beneficiary named in the Will. Therefore, you have no control over the assets after they have been transferred out of your estate.

**Trust-Based Estate Plan** – At some point, a Trust-Based estate plan is needed because of a client's assets, family situation, or estate planning goals. A Trust is a more complex estate planning document, but it has much more flexibility than a Will-Based Plan. When a Trust is used for an estate plan, there is much more control over how the estate's assets are used after death.

As we move towards the right of the estate planning continuum, the estate plan documentation becomes more complex. As an estate planning attorney, I help my clients see where they are on the Estate Planning Continuum™ and determine whether they need a Will-based or Trust-based estate plan.

# ANALYZING YOUR ESTATE

The Probate Asset Analysis Diagram™ is a helpful tool for reviewing your assets and understanding your situation and your goals. This overview shows how assets are currently organized from an estate planning standpoint.

My Probate Asset Analysis Diagram™ has been specifically developed and refined to explain how Estate Planning might impact the estate.

*1* The effect of avoiding Probate.

*2* Determining beneficiary designations that need to be checked and updated.

*3* Identifying potential estate tax issues.

**4** Deciding whether a Will or Trust is needed for the estate plan.

# THE SMITH FAMILY CASE STUDY

The Smith Family is a hypothetical family that I use to explain how estate planning works.

Meet John Smith. He is 75 years old. He has been married to his wife Jane for 50 years. Jane and John have two adult children – Tom and Sally. Tom is 50 years old, and Sally is 48 years old. We won't go into much detail about the Smith Family's dynamics for now. For the purposes of this illustration, we will just keep things very simple.

You can imagine how each client and their family have their own unique circumstances and dynamics – and how that could change what a *Proper* Estate Plan means for them.

For example, maybe Tom and Sally are the ideal children good with money, have stable marriages, and have no issues, and everybody in the Smith Family gets along. Or perhaps, on the other hand, Tom has a drinking problem, and Sally is married to someone that John and Jane don't like. Maybe John and Jane are each in their second marriage, and each has their own kids from a second marriage. Perhaps John has inherited 200 acres of farmland and wants to make sure that Smith Family Farm is inherited by his children someday, yet still provides for Jane during her lifetime.

You can see how these different situations can affect what kind of estate plan John (or Jane) would choose for themselves. For this particular scenario, we will only be talking about John's estate planning documents.

## Estate Planning Questionnaire

The first step is to create a list of assets. We include a questionnaire for our estate planning clients to provide in advance of the first meeting. This information also provides insights into the client's family and a glimpse of John and Jane's estate planning goals.

Here are the assets that John Smith listed on his estate planning questionnaire.

### John Smith Assets

| House | = | $250,000 | John/Jane (Joint) |
|-------|---|----------|-------------------|
| Duplex | = | $200,000 | John |
| Savings | = | $150,000 | John |
| CD | = | $ 20,000 | John/Tom |
| CD | = | $ 20,000 | John/Sally |
| 401K | = | $600,000 | John (Jane Bene) |
| Car | = | $ 20,000 | John |
| Hse Itms | = | $ 5,000 | John/Jane |
| **Total Value =** | | **$1,265,000** | |

You can see from the John Smith Asset list that he has
an estate worth $1,265,000.00. Some of John's assets are
owned jointly with Jane. Some assets are held only in John's
name. And some assets have beneficiary designations
associated with them.

# PROBATE ASSET ANALYSIS DIAGRAM FOR JOHN SMITH

It's hard to analyze anyone's estate when their assets are not
organized for estate planning purposes. To more effectively
analyze the assets of John's estate, we take this information
and turn it into the Probate Asset Analysis Diagram™. Here is
John Smith's Probate Asset Analysis Diagram™:

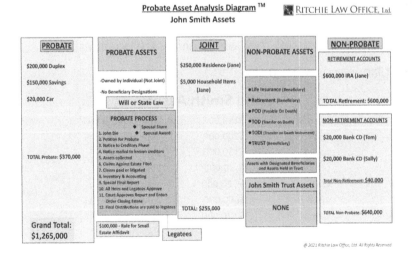

The Generational Wealth System

On the very left-hand side of the diagram, there is a column named "Probate Assets". In the middle of the diagram is a "Joint Asset" column. On the right-hand side is a "Non-Probate Assets" column. I will explain what each of these columns means and how they are important to the estate planning process through the Smith Family Case Study.

All assets that you own can be categorized in one of three ways for estate planning purposes. An asset can be considered:

*1* A Non-Probate Asset

*2* A Jointly Owned Asset, or a

*3* A Probate Asset

# NON-PROBATE ASSETS

The first category is what I call the Non-Probate Assets. You'll find these assets listed on the right-hand side of the probate asset analysis diagram. These are assets that either:

*1* Have beneficiary designations associated directly with the account or asset itself; or

*2* Assets held in the name of a Trust.

Assets that have beneficiary designations will easily transfer upon death to the named beneficiary.

In our example, we have two $20,000.00 CDs. John has named Tom as the beneficiary of one CD and Sally as the beneficiary of another CD. John also has a 401k, which he has named his wife Jane as the beneficiary.

Upon John's passing, one CD will be transferred to Tom, the other CD will be transferred to Sally, and the 401k will be transferred to Jane because they have been named as beneficiaries of those respective accounts.

The types of accounts and assets that have direct beneficiary designations available to them are as follows:

1 Retirement accounts;

2 Life insurance policies;

3 Bank accounts;

4 Brokerage accounts;

5 Your Personal Residence via a "TODI"

Illinois and many other states also allow a beneficiary to be named for a personal residence. In Illinois, this can be accomplished through a "Transfer on Death Instrument" or "TODI".

The Transfer on Death Instrument is a deed-like document. It looks very similar to a deed that you receive when you purchase a home, except in the TODI there is additional language that states upon your passing, your home will be automatically transferred to the beneficiaries you name in the document. The TODI is only available for a personal residence. It cannot be used for other real estate beyond the primary residence.

For example, if John and Jane own their home jointly (which they do), they could sign a TODI and name Tom and Sally as the beneficiaries of their home. This makes sure that their home will automatically be transferred to Tom and Sally upon the last of John and Jane to die and **AVOID PROBATE.**

*Key Concept – TODI: The TODI document is usually prepared by an attorney when they are preparing other estate planning documents for their clients. TODI's may be called by other names in other states and may have different requirements to be valid. In Illinois, this document has to be signed in front of two witnesses and a notary. This document also must be recorded like a deed. A validly signed and recorded TODI will name beneficiaries for a home and make sure it avoids Probate.*

**Trust Assets** – Any asset or account held in the name of a Trust is a Non-Probate Asset as well.

As I previously discussed, a Trust is an agreement between three parties:

The first party is called the Grantor. The Grantor is the person that signs the Trust Agreement and by signing the Trust Agreement – they create the Trust.

The second party is the Trustee. A Trustee is the person named in the Trust to be the manager of the assets in the Trust. A Trustee's job is to review the Trust Agreement and to make sure the assets are being managed in a way that reflects the Grantor's wishes. The Trustee is the person that can sign on behalf of the Trust. The Trustee is the one that decides when distributions should be made to the beneficiaries of the Trust.

The third and final party to a Trust is the beneficiary of the Trust. A beneficiary is the person or group of people named in the Trust who are supposed to benefit from the assets in the Trust. They can receive the principal in the Trust and/or the income generated from the assets of the Trust.

Also, as I have previously mentioned earlier in this chapter, a *Revocable Living Trust* is a type of Trust where the language within the Trust Agreement states that the Grantor can amend or even revoke (terminate) the Trust if they want to. So that means they can take all the assets out of the Trust and terminate that Trust if they don't want the Trust anymore.

An Irrevocable Trust is a Trust where the language in the Trust Agreement states that once the Grantor signs the Trust Agreement and creates it, they cannot change the terms of that Trust.

**Key Concept – Trusts:** *Because Trust Agreements name their own beneficiaries, any asset in a Trust will automatically have a beneficiary assigned to it. As a result, any asset in a Trust is a Non-Probate Asset because these assets will avoid Probate and easily transfer to the beneficiaries named in the trust agreement.*

**Key Concept – Non-Probate Assets:** *It is important to remember that – Non-Probate Assets are assets or accounts that have beneficiary designations directly associated with them – such as life insurance, retirement accounts, bank accounts, brokerage accounts, and TODIs. Non-Probate Assets are also assets held by a Trust and designated to be transferred to the Beneficiaries named in the Trust Agreement. Either way, they will avoid Probate because these assets have beneficiary designations associated with them (because of being in a Trust or because of direct beneficiary designations).*

# JOINTLY OWNED ASSETS

The second category of assets for estate planning purposes is Joint Assets. Joint Assets are assets that John and Jane own together as joint owners with right of survivorship.

Many times, married couples will own cars, their home, bank accounts, and other assets as "joint tenants with right of survivorship". This means that upon John's passing, Jane will automatically inherit those assets as a matter of law through the joint ownership designation. No paperwork has to be filed or claims made – the assets just automatically transfer to Jane's at the time of John's death.

You don't have to be married to own an asset jointly with another person. Anybody can own an asset jointly with another person, and the asset will automatically transfer to the surviving joint owner upon the first joint owner to die.

If you look at our Probate Asset Analysis Diagram™, you will see in the jointly owned category that John and Jane own their home and their household items as joint tenants with right of survivorship.

**Key Concept – Joint Assets:** *The rule with Joint Assets is that these assets will automatically go to the surviving joint owner after the first joint owner passes away. If there is no surviving owner, these assets DO NOT automatically transfer because there is no joint owner to automatically transfer to. In this case, these assets will become "Probate Assets" and may then have to go through the court process of Probate to be transferred to their heirs.*

**Key Concept – Joint Assets:** *Note that Joint Assets can also have beneficiary designations associated with them. Upon the first joint owner passing, the Joint Asset will automatically transfer to the surviving joint owner. Upon the second joint owner passing, the asset will then be transferred to the named Beneficiary. Often, married couples will own an asset jointly and also name their children (or their Child's Trust) as the beneficiary of the Joint account. Because of the beneficiary designation, the asset will be transferred through the beneficiary designation and not be transferred through Probate.*

*For example, John and Jane had a bank account with $20,000.00 in it, and that account was jointly owned with right of survivorship. John and Jane also named Tom and Sally as beneficiaries of that joint bank account as well. Upon John's passing, Jane would automatically inherit that account. If Jane had predeceased John or if John and Jane both died simultaneously, then the bank account would be transferred to Tom and Sally through the beneficiary designation.*

# PROBATE ASSETS

Our third estate plan category are "Probate Assets". You can think of Probate Assets as all other assets in John Smith's Estate that don't fit into the "Joint Asset" category or the "Non-Probate" category.

Probate Assets are assets that:

**1** Are only owned in one person's name (not jointly owned with anyone else); AND

**2** Do Not have beneficiary designations.

Because Probate Assets are not controlled by joint ownership and do not have beneficiary designations, they **DO NOT automatically transfer upon someone's death.**

When we have Probate Assets in someone's estate, we have to ask ourselves two questions:

**Question 1: Who is going to inherit these Probate Assets?** We do not have beneficiary designations telling us who is supposed to inherit these assets. Likewise, we do not have joint ownership telling us who inherits these assets.

**Answer:** The Will is the document that states who will inherit the Probate Assets.

**Question 2: How are these Probate Assets going to**

**be legally transferred from the estate to Legatees or Heirs?** Legatees are people named in a will. If someone doesn't have a Will, then their state's laws will say who their heirs are. Heirs are people that inherit through state law.

**Answer:** Probate Assets are transferred either through the Court Process of Probate or through a Small Estate Affidavit.

**Transferring Probate Assets in Illinois** – There are two ways to transfer Probate Assets in Illinois – through the Court Process of Probate or through a Small Estate Affidavit. As these rules are all state-specific, it is highly recommended that you speak to an estate planning attorney about the specific rules in your state for Probate and Small Estate Affidavits. While the laws are subject to change, I'll provide a very general overview of the current Illinois rules.

**The Court Process of Probate** – The first way that Probate Assets can be transferred is through the court process called Probate. The Probate Court is where we get the term "Probate Assets" and "Non-Probate Assets". Probate Assets may have to go through the court process of Probate in order to be transferred from your estate to your legatees or heirs at law. In contrast, Non-Probate Assets will never have to go through Probate because beneficiary designations or joint ownership will transfer those assets directly.

In Illinois, the Probate process takes about one year to complete if there are no complications. According to Illinois Probate law, the following steps must be completed before all assets of a Probate Estate can be distributed to the heirs and/or legatees.

1  John Smith dies

2  Petition for Probate is filed

3  Notice to unknown creditors is published

4  Notice mailed to known creditors

5  Estate assets collected by executor

6  Claims against estate filed by creditors

7  Claims paid or denied by executor

8  Inventory & accounting of estate assets by executor

9  Special final report to court by executor

10  All heirs and/or legatees approve accounting and report

11  Court approves report and enters order closing the estate

12  Assets are distributed to heirs and/or legatees

You can see all of the steps that Illinois Probate Law requires to be completed from the time John Smith passes away in Step 1 until John Smith's Probate Assets can be distributed in Step 12.

It's a lengthy process primarily due to the six-month creditor claim period. It's required to notify any potential creditors of John Smith's estate of John Smith's death by publishing a notice in the local paper and directly mailing a notice to any known creditors of John's estate.

Once the notice to creditors in the newspaper is published, creditors have 6 months to file a claim against John's estate. Even if there are no creditors of John's estate, Illinois law still requires this process.

**Key Concept – Probate:** *Most people want to avoid Probate for their estate because of how long it takes to get through. The other reason people want to avoid Probate is because it is a public process. Various reports and accountings must be filed with the Court and anyone can look in the court file and review those documents. Avoiding Probate allows the details of your Probate Assets and Estate Plan to remain private.*

**The Small Estate Affidavit** – The second (and much easier) way to transfer Probate Assets in Illinois is through something called a Small Estate Affidavit. Illinois passed this law allowing Probate Assets of "small estates" to be transferred by signing a special statutory affidavit in order to save the court's time.

A "small estate" is defined as any Probate Estate that has less than $100,000 of Probate Assets. Note that Non-Probate

Assets and Jointly Owned Assets are not considered when calculating the Probate Asset total.

For example, John could have a one-million dollar life insurance policy that has a named beneficiary — which is a Non-Probate Asset.

This one-million dollar policy is not an asset in the Probate Asset Category on the Probate Asset Analysis Diagram. Therefore, it is not used to determine if a Small Estate Affidavit can be used to transfer John's Probate Assets.

The Small Estate Affidavit is a statutory form. In summary, the Small Estate Affidavit states that:

**1**   John Smith passed away.

**2**   John's total Probate Assets is less than $100,000.

**3**   John Smith had a Will (If John did not have a Will, it would state that Illinois Law would be followed for the distribution of John's Probate Assets).

**4**   John Smith's Will distributed all of his assets to his children because his spouse has predeceased him (or other bequests his Will may have stated).

**5**   Assets in John's Probate Estate should be distributed equally to John's children or other beneficiaries as named in the Will.

Anybody can sign a Small Estate Affidavit on behalf of John's estate to transfer any of John's Probate Assets. Usually, a close relative would be the person to sign a Small Estate Affidavit, but it could be a close friend or someone else familiar with John's assets and estate.

In our example, Tom or Sally could complete and sign the Small Estate Affidavit. They attach John's death certificate and a certified copy of John's Will to the Affidavit. They then give the Affidavit to a bank or other institute that is holding John Smith's Probate Assets.

The institution (including the Secretary of State for vehicle titles) would review and approve this Affidavit. If approved, they would cut checks directly to Tom and Sally or transfer car titles to Tom and Sally.

Any Estate Planning attorney's office should be able to assist with completing Small Estate Affidavits.

**Key Concept – Small Estate Affidavit:** *A Small Estate Affidavit is an easy way to transfer Probate Assets out of someone's estate. In order to qualify to use a Small Estate Affidavit the Probate Assets in a deceased person's estate has to be less than $100,000 (Illinois law). If there is more than $100,000 of Probate Assets in an estate – then the court process of Probate has to be used to transfer those Probate Assets. The court Probate*

*Process takes at minimum one year to complete while a Small Estate Affidavit usually takes a couple of weeks to complete.*

## DETERMINING IF YOU NEED A WILL-BASED PLAN OR A TRUST-BASED PLAN

Utilizing the information provided by the Probate Asset Analysis Diagram™, four important questions must be answered to determine whether a Will-Based Estate Plan or a Trust-Based Estate Plan is needed.

**Question 1: Can Your Estate Avoid Probate Without a Trust?** This is where the Probate Asset Analysis Diagram™ comes in very handy. We can see for sure whether your estate would avoid Probate without using a Trust. In order to avoid Probate without needing a Trust we have to be able to use direct beneficiary designations to transfer assets outside of Probate. In Illinois you can still have some assets in the Probate category as long as the total Probate Asset category is less than $100,000 in value (so a Small Estate Affidavit can be used to Transfer those remaining Probate Assets). Note: Each state has their own rules as to what amount of Probate Assets constitute a "Small Estate".

For married couples we also have to plan for a "worst case scenario" where both spouses die and all of their Joint Assets become Probate Assets. For example, if John and Jane both passed away in a car accident, all of their Joint Assets would transfer to the Probate Asset column of John's Probate Asset Analysis Diagram™. These assets may push his Probate Asset value over $100,000 and necessitate Probate. It is important to plan for this "worst case scenario" as John and Jane would not want their children forced to go through Probate to administer either of their estates.

Suppose there are assets that we cannot name beneficiary designations directly, such as farmland or investment real estate, expensive cars, etc.. In that case, we may need to set up a Trust for John's estate plan and transfer those assets into his Trust. That way, those assets become Non-Probate Assets through the Trust Beneficiaries.

**Question 2: Are Your Net Estate Assets Approaching $4,000,000.00 In Value?** As of the date of this publication Illinois has an estate tax credit of $4,000,000. So, if someone's total estate is worth more than $4,000,000.00 at the time of their death, then their estate will be subject to an Illinois estate tax based upon the total estate amount. As of the date of this publication the federal estate tax credit is $11.7 million per person. If a person's estate is over $11.7 million then their estate will be subject to federal estate tax as well. Note: Illinois and federal estate tax credit amounts are subject to change by their respective legislatures. You should speak to an attorney experienced in estate tax planning for more information.

Many people don't have to worry about the Illinois or federal estate tax as the net value of their estate is not over $4,000,000 for Illinois or $11.7 million for the federal government.

But for those whose estates are approaching over $4,000,000 and are married, we can use a Trust to double the Illinois estate tax credit from $4,000,000 to $8,000,000. We can do this for the federal estate tax credit amount as well and double the total estate tax credit to $23.4 million.

For purposes of estate planning, if your estate is approaching $4,000,000 which includes life insurance policies, retirement accounts and equity in real estate, then you may want to consider a Trust for your estate plan.

## Question 3: Do You have a "Complicated" Family Situation? For estate planning purposes, a "complicated family situation" primarily means having a "blended family."

A blended family is one where there are children from a previous marriage or relationship. For estate planning purposes, there is almost always some sort of conflict between a surviving spouse and children from a previous marriage, even if everyone gets along when it comes to estate planning.

Suppose all estate assets are distributed directly to a surviving spouse through joint ownership. In that case, beneficiary designations, or a Small Estate Affidavit, those assets are now one-hundred percent owned by the surviving spouse. That spouse can do whatever they want to with those assets. Upon their passing, the surviving spouse may or may not provide for the children from a prior marriage.

You may want to leave some money to the children directly through your Will, but Illinois law allows a surviving spouse to claim either one-third or one-half of a deceased spouse's Probate Estate no matter what the deceased spouse's Will says. This is called the "Illinois Spousal Share".

Trusts have the flexibility for a deceased spouse to provide for a surviving spouse for the surviving spouse's lifetime and still control the remaining assets after the surviving spouse dies so that the deceased spouse's children receive an inheritance.

Every family has different dynamics. Proper Estate Planning™ can facilitate wishes to treat all parties in a fair and equitable way. Options include a combination of Wills, Trusts, and Beneficiary Designations.

**Question 4: Do You Want To Ensure Your Children Receive Their Inheritance?** Even if there currently isn't a blended family situation, upon the first spouse passing the surviving spouse may still get remarried later. They could potentially update their Will and change their beneficiary designations to distribute 100% of your/their assets to the second spouse.

Just as a blended family situation, a Trust-Based Estate plan could provide for the surviving spouse and make sure your half of the marital assets are eventually distributed to your children.

# CONCLUSION

This chapter discussed the importance of having a Proper Estate Plan™ and reviewed the steps of analyzing an estate to determine whether a Will-Based Estate Plan or a Trust-Based Estate Plan is most beneficial and why.

As an estate planning attorney, one of my greatest joys is the process we use in counseling clients through the decision-making process used to create a legally binding and **_Proper_** Estate Plan™. This process is instrumental in charting your course and leaving your legacy for future generations.

*Ritchie Law Office, Ltd. creates and updates estate plans for Illinois residents throughout the state. To learn more about the Ritchie Legacy Planning Session™ and the benefits of a Proper Estate Plan™ visit www.ritchielawoffice.com or phone (309) 662-7000.*

# CHAPTER 9

# Tax Strategy

I f we were to ask any worker in the U.S. the significance of April 15th, 'Tax Day' would be their immediate response. We all widely accept that date as the official U.S. deadline for filing federal and state taxes for the previous year.

We know it as a straightforward process where we file a simple form stating last year's income and taxes paid, and then the IRS returns us a huge check! – At least I've heard that's how it works for some people. Yet, all those years I was preparing tax returns for my particular clients, I found that to be the exception rather than the rule.

Most of the people I've worked with have a sense of dread when it comes to filing their taxes. It's a time-consuming process that often requires the help of a professional. It's a paradox that the more our government tries to simplify the tax code and filing process, the more complex it becomes. Up until the final calculations are made, our stomachs are in knots, wondering if we'll actually get a refund or end up owing the IRS a large amount.

While nearly everyone is familiar with Tax Day, very few people know what "Tax Freedom Day" signifies. It's the day of the year where working tax-payers stop working for the government and begin to actually keep the money they toil for. The National Tax Foundation calculates a date based upon the national averages. They start by projecting all federal, state, and local taxes and then divide that by the total personal income for all Americans for the year. Once they have that collective ratio of income to taxes, they can use that percentage and apply it to the days in the year to find our national freedom day. Using this formula, April 17th is our magic number for 2021, after which the average American is free to keep his income for himself. Well, at least until January 1st of the following year.

It absolutely boggles my mind that an average person contributes nearly ten years of his life in service to the government over the span of a thirty-year career! And when they finally retire, the taxes continue to take its toll.

But in the end, when a person arrives at their final resting place, the taxes cease, right? You would hope, but in many cases, what remains is often taxed as it transfers to the rightful heirs.

With the bulk of the tax load placed upon the affluent, it only makes sense they would do what they can to minimize the financial impact. As the old saying goes, "It's not what you make, but what you keep that's important." I would actually take that even a step further and say it's not what you keep, but what you're able to pass on that really makes a difference.

# THE GREATEST THREAT TO YOUR WEALTH

The media loves to decry the loopholes of the uber-wealthy and criticize them for not paying their fair share to the country. Perhaps this is political posturing, based upon carefully selected data to support an opinion. Or maybe the billionaires live under a different tax code than the rest of us? You can decide that for yourself. What you can't argue is that the extremely affluent employ teams of financial advisors, accountants, and attorneys to protect their money. It's because they understand the impact taxes can have on their wealth and the value of investing in professionals to minimize the tax load they'll carry.

To a lesser degree, most affluent people still invest in professional tax preparers every year. Is it surprising people would actually pay to have someone do their taxes when they could do it themselves or even use software such as Turbotax? You wouldn't be surprised at all if you'd seen the costly mistakes and missed deductions as a result of forgoing an experienced tax preparer. And generally speaking, people with complex financial situations understand this. They are fine with paying for a service to simplify their lives with the assurance they are paying the least taxes possible for that year. It makes sense, right? They want to avoid future tax problems and make sure they get every deduction coming. Often, this can save them hundreds of dollars.

And yet, these very same people may be missing a tax liability of comparatively massive proportions! Lack of advanced tax planning within a comprehensive financial plan could potentially cost hundreds of thousands in unnecessary taxes! These long-term liabilities could act as wealth leaches throughout retirement and possibly even continue as a burden to heirs!

So, with stakes so high, why is advanced tax planning often overlooked? In my opinion, it simply comes down to who is providing their investment advice. There are many options when it comes to financial advisors. There are brokers/dealers, insurance professionals, Registered Investment Advisors, online options and many more possibilities for investment or financial advice.

It's common to ask the prospective financial advisor questions about the fees or rates of return on investments. Not bad questions to ask, by any means. We know that fees can erode growth over time, and it's also beneficial to get a decent return within a given risk parameter. But, in my opinion, the rate of return and fees are not the greatest threat to the nest egg! Tax implications can have a far greater impact on wealth, yet many financial advisors fail to address this glaring concern.

Maybe the reason is, the majority of advisors aren't equipped to provide tax guidance! Most are very upfront about this deficiency. Find a brokerage statement, any 401k statement, or even an investment firm's online disclosures often include fine print at the bottom, "its employees and financial advisors cannot provide tax or legal advice. You should consult your attorney or qualified tax advisor regarding your situation. This content should not be depended upon for other than broadly informational purposes. Specific questions should be referred to a qualified tax professional." How can they competently advise on investments when they can't even discuss one of the greatest threats to a family's wealth? Tax planning is a crucial component for a comprehensive financial plan that includes a wealth transfer strategy.

# THREE TAX STAGES

Managing taxation is often about controlling when taxes will be paid on income and investments. We are all familiar with a micro-tax strategy that will focus on minimizing the taxes in the current tax year. But a macro-tax strategy and an extended tax strategy take a more holistic approach that evaluates the long-term tax burden throughout a lifetime and as it passes on to heirs. Part of tax planning is choosing the most advantageous life stage to bear the tax burden on income and assets.

**Micro Taxation, The Employee Stage** – During our earned income years, we often focus on reducing our income taxes for each year. We are assiduous in pursuing any possible deductions and tax credits available. We also contribute to our 401Ks or IRAs, which defers taxes on that income and growth until retirement.

**Macro Taxation, The Retirement Stage** – When facing retirement, taxation can have an even more significant impact on income. In addition, more factors will come into play with retirement account withdrawals, required minimum distributions, social security, and Medicare premiums.

It's a common assumption that taxes will be less in retirement; therefore, it seems beneficial to defer taxes until this stage. But, this is may be far from reality for those with sizeable qualified retirement accounts. In fact, *most* of my clients are shocked when they see their projected tax liabilities! In addition, while we are currently in a low tax environment, that's subject to change. As a result, many will find themselves paying much greater taxes in retirement.

When looking at a macro-tax strategy, we are primarily concerned with the impact of the taxes over the course of a lifetime and how to protect income and growth in retirement.

**Extended Taxation, Wealth Transfer Stage** – Depending on the state and the size of the estate, those without a tax plan could have over half their assets going towards taxes before it reaches their heirs. A number of recent tax changes and new proposals are threatening to dramatically reduce assets passed along.

For starters, January 2020 saw a tax law change that eliminated the stretch IRA that allowed non-spouse heirs to extend tax-deferral benefits of an inherited IRA over a lifetime. Instead, beneficiaries other than a spouse are required to disburse and pay income taxes on such accounts within ten years of the owner's passing.

Another proposal for tax changes includes removing the step-up basis provision, further taxing inherited, non-retirement, investment accounts. Currently, inherited non-retirement assets benefit from a provision that re-adjusts the cost basis of investments, which is the amount that has already been taxed, to the full market value at the time of the owner's death. Such assets are only subject to capital gains above the new valuation instead of the deceased's cost basis. This means if you sell the inherited investment soon after inheriting it, it is likely there won't be a significant gain thereby eliminating a capital gains tax.

Another key provision would include reducing the estate tax exemption by about 50%. Furthermore, we could see an increase in the overall estate tax rate on both a federal and state level.

Those wishing to pass wealth to their family will find an extended tax strategy necessary to protect assets as they are passed from generation to generation.

**Comprehensive Taxation Strategy** – A comprehensive tax plan involves evaluating an individual's financial picture and projecting across all three stages to best meet their goals.

Often of a long-term strategy involves shifting a tax obligation from one stage to another. Sometimes it makes sense to defer taxes. Other times, it is advantageous to settle with paying tax earlier, at a reduced rate, for a greater overall benefit.

# FOUR TAX BUCKETS

I've heard marketing pitches promise a tax-free retirement, but when digging deeper you might find 'tax-free' as misleading. At some point, income taxes were paid. The only saving grace is, we often can decide when we get taxed on our income; tax-free *growth* is a possibility. In addition, there are options for financial vehicles; whether a financial product or a tax vehicle, we can position our funds to be taxed when most advantageous.

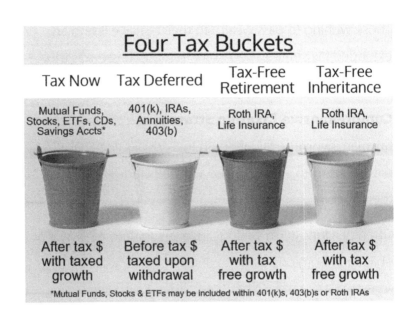

# Four Tax Buckets

| Tax Now | Tax Deferred | Tax-Free Retirement | Tax-Free Inheritance |
|---|---|---|---|
| Mutual Funds, Stocks, ETFs, CDs, Savings Accts* | 401(k), IRAs, Annuities, 403(b) | Roth IRA, Life Insurance | Roth IRA, Life Insurance |
| After tax $ with taxed growth | Before tax $ taxed upon withdrawal | After tax $ with tax free growth | After tax $ with tax free growth |

*Mutual Funds, Stocks & ETFs may be included within 401(k)s, 403(b)s or Roth IRAs

# ETF TAX ADVANTAGES

Exchange-Traded Funds (ETFs) are one investment vehicle offering distinct tax advantages and options for tax planning. ETF investments typically incur fewer capital gains taxes due to how they are structured. Because of the very nature of the funds, there are fewer changes; its passive investment style usually results in less capital gains taxes than a more actively traded portfolio. This is in sharp contrast to mutual funds!

Many mutual fund investors are shocked when they experience capital gains tax, even in a year where there's a decline in their investment's overall market value. This can happen due to changes within a mutual fund's holdings, where stocks held within the fund are sold at a gain. For example, even if an investor did not sell their shares of the fund, those gains within the fund are passed on to the investor as taxable income. An adjustment is then made to the cost basis. I've personally seen this result in tens of thousands of dollars in capital gains for investors.

Even more valuable for controlling taxes is the ETF's mechanism for strategic tax harvesting, using losses to offset capital gains. This is a process where one ETF is sold as a loss for a tax deduction benefit while immediately reinvesting the proceeds in a similar ETF to meet the same investment objectives. Done carefully, wash sale penalties can be avoided. The investor can now sell another security that has capital gain and offset their gain with their loss. As a result, the investor has more control over the capital gains tax they pay.

# A HOLISTIC APPROACH TO GENERATIONAL WEALTH PLANNING

As described in chapter 2, the generational wealth wheel has six clearly defined spokes that connect through a central hub. Tax considerations are the central hub that serves to intertwine all of the components for a holistic generational wealth strategy.

Tax planning may only be one aspect of financial planning, but it encompasses every other element that I've written about. Most all financial maneuvers will ultimately have an impact on the big picture of taxation. Think of this as the tipping of a domino. Each action will trigger another, so we have to look at the end result. When tax implications are taken into consideration for the overall health of the strategy, multiple calculations are required. These various scenarios must be illustrated and compared to determine the overall advantages or disadvantages of any action.

A common question I'm asked, "Is a Roth IRA conversion a good idea?". I understand the question, and it's a great goal to pay the taxes on retirement accounts now before potential future tax hikes. However, it's not an easy yes or no answer because there are so many factors to be considered.

For instance, paying those taxes on retirement accounts in a single year can cause an immediate tax liability that must be factored into the equation. And, if the market is near its peak, those accounts have experienced growth and will cause the immediate tax liability to be more significant. Furthermore, those immediate taxes paid are potential investment funds that will no longer exist to benefit from future market growth. Finally, when converting, there's the matter of choosing the investment vehicle that will provide the most advantageous long-term benefit for retirement and heirs.

A Roth IRA conversion may certainly be beneficial, but it's not a change I'd recommend without calculating all scenarios to weigh the possible tax advantages against the larger picture. There are numerous tax maneuvers that cause ripple effects leading to near limitless outcomes. I certainly don't wear a cape, but in this regard, I relate to the character Dr. Strange in the movie *Avengers: Infinity War*. In one epic scene he uses his magical Time Stone to calculate millions of possible future outcomes to find the only course of events that defeats the villain Thanos. But, instead of using a magical Time Stone, I'm armed with various financial software tools that run scenarios in choosing the best path.

Every individual has a unique situation, and every piece of their financial position impacts the entire financial picture. As such, no individual investment, transaction, or financial strategy can exist in a bubble but must fit as part of the long-term plan to achieve goals. A complete financial plan must include income distribution planning, Social Security filing options, tax strategies, increased healthcare costs, inflation adjustments, and estate legacy planning. Each of these individual items is inseparable from the others in how they impact the overall financial picture. Therefore, a financial plan's recommendations are often complex and strategically balanced.

Comprehensive financial planning is a holistic approach, integrating all financial components, including taxes, towards an efficient wealth transfer strategy.

### References

1. https://mcbeathfinancialgroup.com/blog/tax-free-retirement/
2. https://mcbeathfinancialgroup.com/blog/save-taxes-in-retirement/
3. https://www.thebalance.com/what-is-tax-freedom-day-3306327
4. https://www.edwardjones.com/us-en/client-resource-center/tax-statements-resources/tax-resources
5. https://www.investopedia.com/explaining-biden-s-tax-plan-5080766

CHAPTER TEN

# Your Wealth Advisory Crew

Some of my fondest childhood memories were of my father gently steering our family pontoon, the SS Minnow across beautifully calm Minnesota lake waters. What great summers we had with him as our captain and the rest of the family as the crew. (It was our job to pack the sandwiches and fill the cooler with sodas!) I don't remember having a care in the world in those simpler times.

But operating a water vessel isn't always as easy as steering a boat and enjoying the day. For some, it's a career choice with shipping across the dangerous high seas. And others put their life on the line while serving in our US Coast

Guard. The nerve-wracking portrayal of the most daring Coast Guard rescue in history is a harrowing reminder of the dangers they both face and the skills needed for survival. (Spoiler Alert! The following few paragraphs reveal some plotlines from the 2016 film, *The Finest Hours*.)

A historically savage nor'easter storm unleashed its fury on the New England coast on a frigid February day in 1952. Waves over sixty feet high battered a recently repaired SS Pendleton. Still, the oil tanker may have survived the storm's fury if only the captain had heeded the engineer's advice. Unfortunately, disaster struck, and their only hope for survival was the valiant expertise of the remaining ship crew. They were rescued only by the miraculous heroics of a team of four valiant coastguardsmen in a small motor lifeboat. The skill and nerve of this team in navigating such treacherous waters are what makes this story legendary!

Watching this movie, I was particularly captivated by a few details that might serve as lessons for us all.

First, storms are going to happen, and they are unpredictable. I think we can all agree that's generally the way life is as well. So, it helps to be as prepared as possible. By some accounts, the shoddy welding job on the doomed tanker shouldn't have passed inspections. It wasn't in condition to weather the storm. Likewise, when it comes to financial and legacy plans, it's not only important to be prepared but to have adequate inspectors. Many times, I've personally discovered huge holes in estate plans *prepared by attorneys!* I've seen well crafted estate plans that are ineffective and unfunded. I'm not saying that the attorney created a flawed plan, but there are significant steps that need to be taken in order for the plan to work! Unfortunately, it isn't the attorney's role to help the client change all of their financial documents and designations in order for the plan to work. And trust me, it is a lot of work! In such cases, it's been necessary to recommend, and help my clients with, substantial 'repairs' to help my clients reach their intended destinations.

The second detriment to the SS Pendleton was the fact that the captain did not listen to his crew when they advised he slow his speed. Disaster may have been averted if he'd only trusted those with the expertise in the matter. I believe we all need to be the captain of our own financial ship while seeking the advice of trusted advisors along the way.

"He doesn't listen to anyone anyway.", was said about the ill-fated captain of the SS Pendelton. As a result the crew under his command were left in peril to avert the disaster he left behind. It's easy for me to see the similarities to a well-meaning head of household that fails to seek or heed advice regarding financial protection for their family. In such cases, if something should happen, the family can be left scrambling to pick up the pieces.

And that's precisely what the heroic guardsman's fiancé did! She lept into action when she realized the danger and rallied the townspeople to light up the coast as a beacon for the lost boat to find its way home! It reminds me of the wives that are often the driving force of establishing a relationship with a financial planner. It's still very common for men to handle the finances and investments themselves, which is fine…until something happens.

It's an interesting contrast later in the movie when the Coast Guard rescue boat captain makes a firm decision to STOP listening to his commanding officer! After realizing his superior's orders had nearly gotten them killed, he eventually follows his instincts and turns off his radio! Likewise, we must not be complacent in ensuring our financial professionals are guiding us in the right direction. While it's vital to have advisors, the quality of the advisor definitely makes a difference.

Out of everything, what really had a lasting impact was the teamwork necessary for the successful rescue mission. While on the broken tanker, a variety of different personalities came together towards a common goal. Several of these shipmates had their unique skill that played an essential role in their survival. A team working together towards a common goal is necessary. It's no different when it comes to wealth management.

## THE ESSENTIAL CREW

I don't fault anyone for taking a 'Do-It-Yourself' approach to their investments and financial matters while still working and accumulating funds in their retirement accounts. At this stage, often, their employer's 401K plan makes it simple to chose an adequate investment mix. They may also be okay with selecting investments online or investing with a broker.

But when facing retirement, the stakes become much higher. It's a turning point from the accumulation stage to the distribution phase. With assets reaching their peak, the risks can be greater than ever before. Livelihood in retirement, a spouse's security, and heirs are dependent upon these un-replenishable accumulated investments. A team of essential professionals can help bring all of the various pieces together to provide a perfectly balanced lifestyle, safety for the spouse, and ultimately a lasting legacy.

It's the responsibility of the captain of the financial ship to assemble the 'crew' needed to launch and navigate the financial course towards preservation of lifestyle and legacy. These professionals can be invaluable as a personal advisory board.

**Financial Planner** – Charting the course is the financial planner. A highly qualified financial planner with estate planning experience is a great place to start. This individual can act as the hub in connecting the other pieces together.

*Cautionary Note: Many professionals call themselves Financial Planners, but is the title commensurate with the service provided? It's wise to work with a professional holding a ChFC®or CFP® designation.*

**Investment Advisor** – Once a financial planner creates an overall plan, an investment advisor will work towards keeping the plan on target on an ongoing basis. They are instrumental in selecting investments to fit the plan as well as adjusting through individual needs and market fluctuations.

**Insurance Professional** – Life insurance, long-term care insurance, disability, and possibly annuities will be necessary for a generational planning process. These financial products should fit cohesively within the entire plan for optimum performance.

**Tax Advisor** – A long-term tax strategy will be an essential part of a financial plan and estate transfer plan. A proficient tax planner can leverage the tax code to efficiently direct asset management and wealth transfer.

**Certified Public Accountants or Enrolled Agents** – Either a CPA or an EA can provide tax guidance and assist in tax matters during a wealth transfer. In addition, either one can be valuable as an additional advisor to provide ongoing advice and implement a Tax Advisor's plan.

**Estate Planning Attorney** – An estate planning attorney is essential to legally establish safeguards to protect wishes in the distribution of assets. This attorney will collaborate in creating the necessary trusts and other legal documents necessary for advantageous wealth transfer.

**Executor** – Upon death, an executor is responsible for handling all the final financial affairs to facilitate the wealth transfer in accordance with established legal documents. While this is often a trusted attorney, the testator of the will can choose anyone they wish.

**Trustee** – A trustee is a fiduciary with the responsibility of handling the financial matters of an established trust. Establishing this relationship will be especially important when minor children or other dependants are part of the equation to ensure their protection and your wishes for them are honored upon passing.

## BRINGING THE TEAM TOGETHER

Finding a team that can work together cohesively towards an individual's goals is a must with this many professionals involved. When one individual or firm fills multiple roles, it helps to simplify matters when plotting the course and navigating. It's also helpful for heirs to have one central contact to guide them in the right direction when the time comes.

Bringing all the pieces together isn't as difficult as it may sound, but it is a process. Typically with my firm, it begins with someone contacting me about financial planning. I'd recommend seeking a financial planner that has experience with estate planning and tax planning. My background includes years of tax preparation experience and estate planning that guides me as I create the plan. Even as a tax planner, there are times when I may need to consult with a CPA or an Enrolled Agent (EA). An EA is the highest credential awarded by the IRS. Fortunately, I have the convenience of a great accounting Firm, American Tax and Accounting, which is only two doors down from my office!

I also have a foundation in insurance, so I'll assess risks and look for opportunities where insurance products might fill those needs. Often my financial planning clients will already have life insurance as part of my portfolio, but I'll assess the existing policy to find if it might benefit from adjustments.

I'm also usually chosen to be the permanent investment advisor after the plan's creation. It only makes sense that my clients would choose me to execute the plan I created. I'll understand my client's goals better than anyone and the family will have one point of contact for all financial matters when needed.

As a comprehensive financial planner, I also take an active role in setting a foundation for estate planning and wealth transfer strategies. Yes, I'll definitely refer to an attorney I work with for the legal side, but the financial aspect is certainly my responsibility.

I'll work hand-in-hand with an estate planning attorney. Often, Chad Ritchie and I will collaborate via email and phone to establish the estate plans necessary for our clients. I also have complete confidence in Chad to act as an executor of an estate and to recommend a trustee when needed.

# SELECTING THE RIGHT TEAM MEMBERS

Yes, I recommend starting with a financial planner as a hub to tie everything together. However, many people have a pre-existing relationship with an accountant, attorney or another financial professional. That's fine, and I often work with other professionals as part of the team. Other times, attorneys and accountants will refer their clients to me in order to provide a holistic plan for them. The important thing is open communication within the team to assist their shared client.

When it comes to choosing a financial advisor, I can speak from experience on what to seek.

**Focused On Your Goals, Not Products** – I'd recommend choosing a fee-based or fee-only financial planner who will incorporate a holistic approach to investing. Many firms may be quick to recommend products instead of focusing on how to best achieve a client's goals, first and foremost. Some firms, such as my own, are considered fee-based. The reason we classify this way is because we have the ability to use life insurance for our clients who are looking for wealth transfer and protection options for their family. All life insurance compensation is commission based, paid by the insurance carrier. Therefore, since fees are not charged on those products, we are not considered fee-only. However, planning and investment advisory services are strictly based on fees, not commissions.

**Fiduciary** – Not all financial advisors are required to act in the best interest of their clients. Only Registered Investment Advisors are bound by the Investment Advisers Act of 1940 to act with the highest integrity in serving in their client's best interest. A fiduciary has the highest standards in ethics and is bound to act in the best interest of their clients.

**Concierge Service** – Choose a firm that can provide personalized service and ongoing support with a focus on existing clients. An established relationship will be at the core of the planning process.

Seek an exclusive firm that specializes in working with people similar to yourself. When choosing a highly regarded individual advisor, it's important to know they have a contingency plan and support available to provide ongoing service over the long term. Most independent boutique firms are supported by much larger organizations that offer support on the back-end. It can be helpful to be acquainted with who else may be part of servicing their clients.

**Advanced Software Tools** – Advanced programs give an

edge in the planning process, and the detailed reporting helps provide clarity and confidence in estate plans. While many firms utilize sophisticated financial software programs to assist in the planning process, not all methods are the same. Even using the same software, it's the expertise of the user that makes the difference. It's very similar to letting a novice play on a Steinway grand piano. It may be the finest piano made, but if all the user can play is 'Mary Had a Little Lamb,' it's a waste.

Also, many firms will provide Wealth Management Tools that go way beyond simply accessing account balances. You should expect to have financial information accessible in one place, automatically updating in real-time for secure online goal tracking.

**Experience** – Education, and letters behind the name are great, but experience is the greatest teacher. The proficiency required for financial planning encompassing an estate plan is best suited for someone with more than a decade of experience. Conversely, too much experience may be an issue if the advisor isn't tech-savvy or if the age means he or she may no longer be in practice when most needed.

**Remote Capable** – When selecting an advisor, find someone comfortable with meeting needs remotely.

Some decide to move out of state, become a snowbird, or frequently travel. Or perhaps it's convenient to have an advisor capable of collaborating with out-of-town children when the need arises. The tech-savvy advisor can host video conferences and provide service from anywhere in the country. As a result of the Coronavirus, many find it more convenient to meet via zoom calls, regardless of where they live!

# VETTING A FINANCIAL PROFESSIONAL

I'm often mystified when I see a local facebook group post where someone asks a community of complete strangers to recommend a financial advisor. And the community blindly responds with a barrage of dozens of names of various types of local guys that are "great"! Since these strangers have no idea of the original poster's needs or financial status, how is this an effective way to find the help needed? Don't get me wrong, I'm all for referrals, but it might be better if the referral came from someone you knew, trusted, and had experienced similar needs.

Without such a referral, even a quick google search for "Financial Planner" might be a good starting point. Ignoring the paid ads, the local search map usually highlights the top three local firms, which web data suggests are the best matches. From there, examining the content of their websites can help narrow the search.

Finally, I'd recommend utilizing a few other sources that can assist in cross-checking a financial advisor.

**Broker Check** – Brokercheck.finra.org is a free website for searching relevant information on investment advisors, investment firms, and brokerages. It's a background check available at your fingertips. Pay close attention to any possible disclosures.

**Better Business Bureau** – If curious about the rating of a firm based upon customer feedback and complaints, the BBB might be worth a quick check.

**Google** – A quick google search of a firm name and the advisor should show a multitude of results. A robust online presence is a sign of an established advisor.

**Online Reviews** – Most advisors won't have personally shared testimonials or reviews from their clients due to industry regulations. However, unbiased review sites such as google, yelp, or facebook are recommended as independent third-party sources.

# ADVICE FROM THE "EXPERTS"

It seems everywhere you turn, a financial guru is spitting out money advice, and I want to offer a word of caution concerning such. First, it's prudent to filter all such advice, discern what qualifications they have earned, question if they have an agenda driving the information, and if the advice is actually the best for your financial situation.

We are bombarded with people telling us how to handle our money, whether online with Facebook ads, news articles, television programming, and especially on the radio! I recently took a 3 hour trip and heard five different financial "experts" as I tuned into various radio stations along the way. Each one had contrasting advice about how you should handle your personal finances for investments and retirement. Many of the talking points were directly contrary, based upon what they were trying to sell. As an industry insider, I'm entirely aware these 'radio shows' are paid promo spots so that they can push their financial product. I also realized that I would have been very confused if I didn't have my expertise as an investment advisor.

This is an interesting phenomenon. I don't want to completely discredit these talk show hosts. They are clearly educated and can offer thoughtful perspectives. However, their sound bites and catchphrases can be detrimental when they evoke an emotional, financial decision. Radio and TV "experts" don't have a personal relationship with the people they are dispensing advice to. It's easy to say what the masses *should* do and how things *should* work, but it's not feasible for everyone to take that advice to heart and aptly apply it to their lives. When receiving any financial advice, it's judicious to consider the source, whether radio, online, or television.

Here are some of the most common sources of financial advice.

**Self-Proclaimed National Gurus** – I agree, Dave Ramsey and Suze Orman have great common sense when it comes to money, and they provide interesting programming.
But they don't know you from Adam, yet they're very comfortable telling you what to do with your money. And by the way, neither of them has a single investment credential.

**Local Radio and Dinner Seminar Hosts** – Local advisors often pay radio stations or buy expensive dinners in order to dispense their financial advice. As mentioned above, It's a marketing expense paid for by selling products to their audience. The advice may or may not be valid, but take heed that it may be one-sided and sales-oriented.

**Robo Advisors** – With no human interaction, an automated algorithm provides asset allocation advice based upon a questionnaire the customer completes. I'm not sure this can even be considered financial advice when it's this impersonal. It's frustrating enough just dealing with an automated phone system when trying to talk to a live person with your cable company or phone company. While a computer algorithm may be able to recommend investments, it most likely will fall far short when it comes to providing an overall financial strategy.

**Employer Sponsored Financial Services** – Some employers will provide a financial services company at little or no cost to help with goals-based planning. It's a nice perk but lacks the personalized approach, as well as the quality and depth provided by retaining your own professional counsel.

**Brokerage Firms** – Brokerages are typically commission-based and do not follow the fiduciary standard. This means if it's in their best interest to promote a proprietary product, they are free to do so, even if it's not in the client's best interest. While these companies may be adequate for simple investments during the accumulation phase, they may not provide the strategy necessary when transitioning into retirement and wealth transfer stages.

**Annuity Specialists** – It may be challenging to spot them immediately, but many financial advisors are simply annuity specialists, carrying only an insurance license. Annuities may be a great product, but if an 'advisor' only specializes in 'safe money solutions,' they're selling without regard for how it fits into your financial plan.

Along the same lines are the insurance agents who might be captive for a specific insurance company. With all due respect, if they can only sell you a company product, how can they truthfully tell you that that product is what is in your best interest?

**The Annuity Haters** – You may have heard the phrase, "I Hates Annuities", by Ken Fisher. Fisher Investments is one of the largest national Registered Investment Advisor Firms, so it's not surprising he doesn't recommend his competitors' products! But what if insurance-based products are the best solution for the client?

Fisher Investments loves to boast about being a fiduciary, their tailored portfolios and no commissions. Of course, they are fee-based, or as they say, "When their customers do better, they do better." They charge a percentage of the assets they manage for their clients. I recommend this model for investors also. But amusingly, Fisher Investments portray themselves as unique in these features! But the reality is, there are tens of thousands of similar SEC and State Registered Investment Advisor Firms, including my own Investment Firm! While the majority of us share the same business model in this regard, many firms such as my own, have a specialized niche to better serve their particular clientele.

With all of these sources, the main question you need to ask yourself is, are you being consulted or are you being sold when seeking direction?

When choosing a professional guide, recognize the potential bias and the philosophy of the person you seek advice from. Not every advisor is the same, and not every advisor has the same goal or path for achieving their client's most desirable outcome.

# INTRODUCING THE NEXT GENERATION

Inviting the next generation into your advisory team may be the most difficult step of all. I've been surprised again and again by how many times grown children haven't a clue about the vastness of their parent's estate.

Sometimes, the wealthy simply don't know how to approach their children to discuss their estate. It's natural, as none of us know when our time will come, and why bring up a dour subject? Other times, with multiple siblings, perhaps a mixed family, and various personalities and histories, it may be a very difficult subject to broach. There may be fear of stirring up resentment, especially when the conversation may turn towards unequal bequests. Or it just may be a matter of deeply seeded privacy about their finances. Perhaps even they don't want their children making plans for their money before it's passed on to them.

Whatever the reason for reluctance, for a multigenerational wealth plan to be most effective, the grown children should eventually be brought into the planning circle. The heirs should know what to expect and what's expected of them. In addition, it's helpful for them to have a pre-existing relationship with the team of professionals that will eventually assist them with navigating the wealth transfer.

For those finding it difficult to bring the next generation to the table, you don't have to do this alone. If you've chosen the right advisory team, they should offer their expertise and support in facilitating a conversation. Obviously, this is a great way to introduce the next generation to the team they will be working with at some point in the future.

When all your financial plans are in place, you can begin the conversation with your financial advisor. If they are assisting with your wealth transfer strategy, they should be enthusiastic about mediating a meeting with your family members. The advisor may also recommend the attendance of the estate planning attorney as well.

If family members aren't local, an advisor should set up a group zoom meeting for all to be present remotely. Before the meeting, have a one-on-one conversation to provide the advisor with any important family details, anything you don't want to be discussed, and other relevant parameters. Based on this information, the advisor should provide a meeting itinerary. Approve the agenda in advance of the meeting and grant your advisor the authority to oversee the group conversation.

### References

1. https://en.wikipedia.org/wiki/The_Finest_Hours_(2016_film)
2. https://time.com/4197131/the-finest-hours-true-story/

# CHAPTER ELEVEN

# Charitable Support

I remember the Sunday my husband and I settled into our church seats as our pastor walked to the pulpit and began his message. "What will your legacy be?" While this is a serious subject, the congregation laughed when he joked about recording his own eulogy and saying great things about himself. But the message was clear: how can we live our life to the fullest, so we make a lasting impact while we're living? And when we pass, what will people say about us at our funeral?

That same week, John McCain's funeral filled the news. Many words were spoken about the legacy he left behind, but none were more emotional or touching than his daughter's. By all accounts, he lived his life serving God, his country, and his family to the best of his ability. It reflected in everything he did and all he left behind. Whether you agree with his political stances or not, I believe we can find inspiration in his character.

Although very few people will be war heroes and run for the office of President of the United States, the truth is, there are so many unsung heroes. There are people that I meet in my office every week that are making impacts in the world they live in and aren't looking for headlines. Most people will never know, but they work, sacrifice, and take action to make a difference for their families and the causes they believe in. And if you ask the loved ones that surround them at the end, they will tell you they left a legacy every bit as meaningful as those left by the people making news headlines.

Of course, many have basic financial concerns for funding retirement. But for some, there is little danger of depleting their retirement funds, and there's something more that drives them. There's usually an underlying purpose they have beyond their own well-being. Naturally, they want to take care of family. But above that, I've found most people of means to be particularly committed to supporting charitable causes.

While retirement planning is focused on personal needs and the wealth transfer strategies are usually for the family, I consider charitable legacy planning as much more selfless.

## WHY SUPPORT A CAUSE?

At first glance, it might appear out of place to address philanthropical giving in a book specifically about passing wealth to future generations. After all, isn't the whole point to transfer as much wealth as possible? Maybe that's part of it, but I don't believe the two are mutually exclusive. It's entirely possible to leave a legacy with both heirs and a worthwhile charitable enterprise. There are a multitude of reasons why someone might be drawn to support a benevolent organization.

For many, there may be an organization that's been important to them at some point in life. Maybe that organization helped them or a family member at one time. I know many are committed to St. Jude or cancer treatment centers, while others have loyalty to their Alma Mater or their church.

With estate planning and proper projections, we may find the estate is more than sufficient to provide for heirs and still have discretionary funds available for endowments.

It's the right of the benefactor to decide how much he/ she bequests to the next generation. Warren Buffet himself has famously pledged to give 99% of his wealth away instead of keeping it within future generations of his family. Why? We can make our own assumptions, but even so, they still stand to inherit over $2 billion each. I think we can all agree with Warren that they will somehow manage to get by.

Often a philanthropic organization might be included in a will and estate plan as a contingency. During the planning phase, unforeseen events must be taken into account. For example, what happens in the event all designated heirs predecease the benefactor? With no further descendants, charitable causes might be the best option.

Finally, when incorporated into a tax strategy, charitable giving may be quite advantageous! When maneuvered properly, donations can reduce an immediate tax burden as part of a micro-tax strategy. Furthermore, it may be an effective part of a wealth transfer strategy on a macro-level. In this case, philanthropic giving may help reduce the amount of inheritance subjected to estate taxes!

# GIVING WHILE LIVING STRATEGIES

I've already addressed strategies for gifting to heirs in Chapter Seven, but I've reserved charitable donations for this chapter. Although the approaches are different, they often are intertwined as part of a comprehensive financial plan for strategic wealth transfer.

Most of the people I encounter are charitable in their very nature to begin with; whatever benefit they derive as a result of their generosity seems to be secondary to their goal of sharing from their heart. With that in mind, the better we can plan their giving allows us to derive a reciprocated benefit that ultimately can be passed along to family or back to the organization. And, I don't think there's much of a debate of whether most people would prefer to write a check to the IRS or their favorite charity!

Starting with the simplest form of donations, we all know that a contribution to a qualified 501c(3) organization is deductible for that tax year, correct? That's true, but taxpayers don't always receive the full benefit if they are not itemizing their taxes. In addition, there could be limitations based on income.

For married filing jointly in 2021, the standard tax deduction is $25,100, or $27,800 if both spouses are over age 65. So, if qualified deductions, including donations, don't add up to over $25,100 for the year, a tax filer will take the standard deduction. Without other tax deductions, it matters little if the contributions are $600 or $25,099. You'll pay the same tax.

Depending on the sum of contributions, there may be better ways to increase the tax benefits.

**Donor-Advised Fund (DAF)** – A DAF is essentially a vehicle that sets up a 'savings/ investment account' for charitable contributions. You make an irrevocable contribution to a third-party fund, realizing an immediate tax deduction for the year of the gift; the fund invests the money in an account you create, where it grows without being taxed. You can request where the charitable donations from the DAF go, when the funds are paid out, and you have a say in how you want the funds in the DAF invested. At your direction, the DAF makes the donations to non-profits on your behalf and has the legal control over these matters. The charities are still informed the donation was made by you.

First, this is a great vehicle for bundling multiple year's charitable giving into one calendar year. Those who regularly donate a generous amount, but not enough to surpass the standard deduction, may consider a DAF to itemize in the years they wish to contribute for multiple years distribution.

For example, consider a working couple who is tithing $1500 a month to their church. If they were to itemize every year, it would still be less than the standard deduction, so no tax benefit is derived over the $600 above the line deduction. However, if they were to establish a DAF and contribute the sum of three years contributions to it, they would have a $54,000 tax deduction in that tax year. They would then make monthly contributions from their DAF. In addition, any growth within the DAF would also be available for charitable gifts at their discretion.

A DAF might also be a useful tool to lower the taxable income in a year where there was a spike in income.

*Advanced Strategy Tip: Funding the DAF is a tax-deduction. You could use any funds available. BUT, by using appreciated assets in a non-qualified account, you'll also avoid the capital gains on these funds, giving a further tax benefit.*

**Qualified Charitable Distribution (QCD)** – Required Minimum Distributions (RMDs) are forced withdrawals from qualified retirement accounts that begin at age 72. Normally, the withdrawals are taxable events. However, some or all of the RMDs, can be donated directly to a 501(c) (3) organization. The donation amount is excluded from your taxable income, and you are still able to take the higher standard deduction. It's an excellent method for maximizing contributions by donating with pre-tax dollars. Keep in mind that you can also use the QCD to donate more than the required minimum. This is a great strategy if you won't need all of your funds during your lifetime.

*Advanced Strategy Tip: Although RMD's do not begin until age 72, you can begin using the Qualified Charitable Distribution at age 70 1/2.*

**Charitable Remainder Trusts (CRT)** – A CRT or a Wealth Replacement Trust allows the donation of assets to a charity while retaining income rights to the earnings during the donor's lifetime. After the end of the trust term (or death), the remaining trust principle passes to charity, or in some cases, to a family foundation. Also, a CRT could be the designated beneficiary of an IRA as part of an estate planning strategy.

In general, it may be best to fund a CRT with an asset that would produce substantial long-term capital gains tax if sold outside the Trust. After the Trust is executed, the donor may transfer this appreciated, low or non-income-producing asset to the CRT. The CRT can then sell the asset and provide the donor an income for life, for a term of years, or for joint lives. Upon the death of the donor or the donor's named non-charitable-income beneficiary, the remaining trust assets will pass to the charity.

This may effectively reduce estate and income taxes without lowering a family's inheritance when making a significant charitable contribution.

For starters, there's an immediate tax deduction for the present value of the assets placed into the CRT, even though those funds aren't transferred until a future date.

Additionally, since the CRT is tax-exempt, appreciated assets donated will not incur capital gains tax for the donor or the charity. And since the Trust is not taxed on appreciation, it means the recipient's income may increase due to having more tax-free funds in the CRT.

Finally, estate taxes are reduced since the asset placed in the Trust has been removed from the estate.

After the donor's death, the remaining assets in the trust pass to the charity, not to the donor's heirs.

**Advanced Strategy Tip:** *The tax savings produced by the charitable donation and the income generated by the Trust can be used to pay premiums on a life insurance policy owned* *by an irrevocable life insurance trust (ILIT) — sometimes known as a "wealth replacement" trust. The life insurance policy in this Trust replaces the value of the assets that pass to the charity in the CRT. Since the life insurance is purchased and owned by the Irrevocable Trust, the proceeds are free of income tax and estate tax.*

**Charitable Lead Trust (CLT)** – A CLT is the opposite of a CRT in that the cash flow from assets within a specifically created trust is donated to a charity, while the assets are ultimately retained to pass along to a donor's family. These irrevocable trusts are established with guidelines that include a specific charitable organization that will receive a regularly defined income for a specified period of time. At the expiration of the period, the remaining funds are distributed to the defined beneficiary. Often the donor will set the CLT to expire upon their death, so assets pass on to heirs at that time.

The beauty of a CLT is the immediate impact on the charity while realizing various tax benefits. Once again, appreciated assets donated to a charity through a CLT will avoid capital gains taxes. At the same time, there will be an immediate tax deduction in the year it's funded for the full value of the contribution. And finally, the assets held in the Trust can potentially be passed on to heirs free of estate taxes.

The specifics of the tax benefits depend upon if the CLT is designated as a Grantor CLT or Non-Grantor CLT.

In a grantor CLT, the donor will maintain some control over the Trust and is considered the owner for income tax purposes. The grantor will pay capital gains taxes on Trust's income as opposed to the higher, ordinary income tax rate. Often, tax-exempt investments will be chosen within the Trust to further minimize the annual tax liability.

A non-grantor CLT relinquishes grantor trust power. As a result, the Trust is taxed on the income generated by assets within the CLT. However, distributions made to charity offer the ability to offset such income.

# LEAVING A LEGACY STRATEGIES

There are a few different ways to pass along assets to a charity when passing. When set up correctly, they will pass free of probate, and it will not be a taxable event. Furthermore, by leaving money to a charity, you'll reduce the size of your estate, and less money will be subject to estate taxes.

**Bequests** – The most straightforward way to provide for a charity is to designate the organization as a beneficiary in a will or Trust. Please remember that Wills are subject to probate, which is a lengthy and public process. Your heirs could also contest your Will if they feel they should receive more. Using a Trust will avoid probate, making your bequest private.

**Beneficiaries** – Similar to bequests, beneficiaries are designated for retirement and investment accounts, as well as life insurance policies. These beneficiary designations take precedence over those stated in a Will or Trust in the event of a discrepancy. Assets passing through a beneficiary designation pass quicker because there isn't probate or trust administration.

Most financial accounts will allow a primary beneficiary and a secondary beneficiary in the event the primary beneficiary has predeceased. A charity is often chosen as the secondary beneficiary.

**Life Insurance Gift** – While beneficiaries of life insurance can be changed by the owner, gifting the actual policy to a charity, by changing the ownership of the policy, surrenders such rights. Once the ownership and beneficiary is established as a qualified 501(c)(3), the premiums become tax-deductible to the donor. If the donor gives an *existing* policy to a charity, the fair market value of the policy (generally, its full cash value) is allowable as an income tax deduction. Upon the insured's passing, the full death benefit will pass to the charity tax and probate-free. Furthermore, these assets do not contribute towards the amount of the estate tax exclusion.

*Advanced Strategy Tip: If the desire is to divide the estate between heirs and charity, donate qualified IRA funds to the charity. Heirs would be required to distribute funds from an IRA within a 10 year period and pay the taxes on distributions. Designating the charity as the beneficiary of those retirement accounts will have the funds pass to the charity tax-free. In cases where the IRA may be divided between beneficiaries, it may be wise to split the IRA and create separate accounts for each beneficiary.*

# CHOOSING A CAUSE

There are so many worthy causes, and for some, it might be a difficult task to choose which charity to support. For others, it's an easy choice, where they've either benefitted from a particular organization or find their mission one they identify with from personal challenges. A very personal connection to an organization brings a higher level of fulfillment from estate planning that can ultimately benefit such a mission.

Throughout my life, I've been blessed to know and serve so many generous people. They are willing to step up and offer their support when they see a need. They'll tithe at church, make a purchase for a school kid's fundraiser, maybe provide an envelope with some cash for a friend or neighbor in need, and endlessly support various charities with donations. The list goes on, as they feel called to help whatever causes they come across! For such generous souls, it may be hard to narrow down a list. But when it comes to estate planning for charitable support, choosing one, maybe two, is recommended to simplify the process.

When choosing a charity, you'll have choices to make. Sometimes people choose a local organization that might be smaller. The advantage to supporting a smaller 501(C)(3) is that a donation will make a much bigger impact! For example, while a $20,000 donation to the Humane Society of Central Illinois would be a huge windfall for them, such a donation would be a drop in the bucket towards the operational budget of the American Red Cross. On the other hand, larger charities can be great to partner with, and they have resources to help in the giving process!

Even medium-sized philanthropical organizations often have

resources and dedicated staff to assist with planned gifting. One particular organization I have the honor of serving on the board is for The OSF Healthcare Foundation. Starting with their resource center at www.osflegacyofhope.org, they are committed to providing educational tools and support to those that wish to partner with them.

Finally, I want to offer a word of caution for those looking to make the most significant impact. It's wise to take the time to do some quick investigation into where donations might actually go. Many 'charities' actually have incredibly high operational costs and pay directors obscene salaries while offering little actual aid to the cause. A quick search of a charity at www.charitynavigator.org can offer prospective stakeholders some solid insight into the benevolent organization.

## ANOTHER WAY TO GIVE

Financial support will always be needed for worthy organizations, but there's another resource needed that's just as valuable. Organizations need people that are willing to step up and volunteer. The people that give their time and become involved as a volunteer are the very life-blood of a cause. It takes an exceptional level of commitment to become active and work hands-on to make a difference.

There is such a need for volunteers and leaders at all levels across so many philanthropies! And I've been a witness to many that have taken up the mantle and made a difference. Immediately, I think of my dear clients who I see volunteering in the Church bookstore at Eastview Christian Church. Another client of mine actively does fundraising for Faith in Action. And a dear family friend works fervently for a Christian Orphanage in India. I know others volunteer to walk dogs for The Humane Society of Central Illinois, and some are committed to missionary trips with their churches! And yet another I'll never forget is a client who left a legacy of service behind with his years of leadership on the board for Heartland Community College.

What strikes me about every one of these examples is the passion every one of them has for their cause! When they talk about their service, they aren't bragging about what they are doing; they are excited about a mission they get to be a part of! It's given them a purpose and goals that aren't monetarily based!

One of the saddest things that can happen to someone as they enter retirement is their loss of purpose. So many people have their identity wrapped up in their careers.

People who have spent decades pursuing goals find themselves stripped of their jobs and may enter a lackluster period of their lives, lacking direction. Studies have shown post-retirement declines in both physical and mental health, as a result!

However, those I see involved with worthwhile groups radiate with inspiration! By giving their time and energies, they seem to have a renewed vitality through the cause that drives them!

# HEROES

I admire these kind-hearted people who selflessly give their money and/or time to local religious, educational, social, or cultural organizations. They experience the immense satisfaction resulting from giving to others and would do it without expecting anything in exchange. I feel it's a duty to ensure we make the most of their efforts and money.

As you've probably realized, it takes a little work and some planning. It may require specific guidance from qualified tax and legal professionals to maximize the impact. And many of the people I meet with have a heart that makes it worthwhile to them. That's why I see them as heroes leaving a legacy. As Meghan McCain said at her father's funeral, "We don't put our heroes on pedestals just to remember them; we raise them up because we want to emulate their virtues. This is how we honor them, and this is how we will honor you."

## References

1. https://www.irs.gov/newsroom/irs-provides-tax-inflation-adjustments-for-tax-year-2021

2. https://charitylawyerblog.com/2021/02/08/new-limits-on-charitable-deductions-in-2021

3. www.mdmag.com/physicians-money-digest/personal-finance/preserve-tax-deductions-by-using-donor-advised-funds-strategically

4. https://www.investopedia.com/terms/c/charitableleadtrust.asp

5. https://www.schwabcharitable.org/maximize-your-impact/develop-a-giving-strategy/align-your-giving-vehicles/charitable-lead-trust

6. https://www.fidelitycharitable.org/guidance/philanthropy/charitable-lead-trusts

7. https://www.irs.gov/retirement-plans/retirement-plans-faqs-regarding-iras-distributions-withdrawals

8. https://osflegacyofhope.org/?pageID=10

9. https://www.investopedia.com/articles/insurance/10/giving-to-charity-using-life-insurance.asp

10. https://www.wiseradvisor.com/article/consider-splitting-your-ira-323/

11. https://www.osfhealthcarefoundation.org/

12. https://www.nber.org/papers/w12123

# Krista McBeath

Krista McBeath is the founder and CEO of McBeath Financial Group, Landmark Wealth Management, Inc, a Registered Investment Advisory Firm in the State of Illinois. She is also the president of McBeath Tax and Financial Services, LLC, a related company offering insurance services.

Krista is an Investment Advisor Representative, a Chartered Financial Consultant®, a Licensed Insurance Advisor, a Fiduciary, and an experienced tax advisor who specializes in financial planning, investments, and insurance solutions for families.

She has been recognized within her industry with numerous production awards but is most proud of the recognition received by the votes of the community she serves. 2021 marked the fifth consecutive year of being voted the #1 Financial Planner in the Pantagraph Reader's Choice Awards. By the newspaper reader's votes, she was also awarded Best Investment firm for the fourth consecutive year.

Krista's personal insights on financial related matters can be found in her monthly articles published in Healthy Cells Magazine, on her blog at **www.mcbeathfinancial.com/blog** and at **facebook.com/mcbeathfinancialgroup**.

Her faith is the foundation of what she values most: family. She balances her successful career with her home life, guarding her time with her husband Robert and her daughter Jillian. They share a love for Disney, sunny beaches and summer vacations at the family lake cabin outside Park Rapids, MN.

Krista is a board member of the OSF Healthcare Community Council and a member of Eastview Christian Church. In addition, she is an ardent supporter of The Humane Society of Central Illinois and Rutan Children's Home.

All reviews for her book are deeply appreciated and can be left on amazon at this link:

**https://mcbeathfinancialgroup.com/bookreview**

## Contact Information

McBeath Financial Group

203 Landmark Dr, Unit A

Normal, IL 61761

(309) 808-2224

Krista@McBeathFinancial.com

www.McBeathFinancial.com

facebook.com/mcbeathfinancialgroup

# Chad A. Ritchie, Esq.

C had A. Ritchie, Esq. is the founder and sole shareholder of the Ritchie Law Office, Ltd., an Estate Planning Law Firm in Bloomington, Illinois, and serving all of Illinois. The Ritchie Law Office, Ltd. is dedicated to *helping its clients achieve peace and lasting legacy through **proper** estate planning.*

Chad has been practicing law since 2002. He is a lifelong Illinois resident, growing up on a farm just outside of Colfax, Illinois. Chad graduated from Illinois Wesleyan University, cum laude, in 1997 and then graduated from Southern Illinois

University School of Law with honors in 2002.

In 2005, Chad started his own law firm, the Ritchie Law Office, Ltd., which has become a leading estate planning law firm in central Illinois. Chad and his firm have received numerous honors and recognition for their client service.

Chad is married to his wife Kara of more than twenty years. They have two children, Addison and Jackson. When not at the office, Chad enjoys being with his family and attending his children's various school and sporting activities.

For more expert information on Estate Planning, Chad has published several articles on his blog which can be found at **www.ritchielawoffice.com/blog** and also at **facebook.com/ritchielawoffice**.

## Contact Information

Ritchie Law Office, Ltd.

2203 E Empire St, Suite G

Bloomington, IL 61704

(309) 662-7000

info@RitchieLawOffice.com

www.RitchieLawOffice.com

facebook.com/ritchielawoffice

Made in the USA
Coppell, TX
29 April 2022